Learn C# Qui

A Complete Beginner's Guide to Learning C#, Even if You're New to Programming

{CodeQuickly}

CodeQuickly.org

ISBN: 978-1-951791-37-7

Free Bonus + Source Code

Programming can be hard if you don't avoid these 7 biggest mistakes! Visit codequickly.org/bonus to get this free PDF guide, and gain access to the source code for all of our books.

codequickly.org/bonus

Contents

Note From the Publisher

If you notice any inaccuracies in the book or links that don't work, please contact us at: support@codequickly.org.

Please put the words "BOOK ERROR" in the subject line, and we'll make sure to make changes and send you a small gift for your input.

Chapter 1: Introductory Topics

C# is an object-oriented programming language with enormous community support since it was built by Microsoft. C# is used for various software development such as Web Applications, Desktop Applications, Mobile Applications, etc.

1.1 - Introduction

Programming is the process of writing instructions for a computer to follow. The instructions will normally be processed by a program named a compiler. The compiler will translate the instructions into a language that the computer can actually read and understand. The compiler for C# is divided into two parts. The first part translates the source code to an abstracted machine code (Intermediate Language) and saves the file to the disk. The second part translates this abstracted machine code into a language that the processor of a specific machine can understand. Often times these two parts of this process are separated by time and space, while other times they are done nearly at the same time. This gives the .Net and C# ecosystem some significant flexibility.

Many people may get frustrated when learning programming for the first time. Do not be. Some people who been programming for a long time get frustrated at times when learning new programming concepts. Feel free to experiment with the samples provided in this book and create new programs. If you get stuck or come across a "road block" just revisit this book again, attempt to search the internet for the answer, or even ask someone who has some programming experience.

The next few subsections will describe common definitions to some programming terms.

1.2 - Variable

A variable is a location in the memory of a program that can have its value change at various times while the program is running. A variable can have any data type that is already defined by the programming language or defined by the programmer(s).

1.3 - Data Types

Every variable in the program must belong to some data type. A data type is a specific kind of data that a computer can represent. A few examples of data types are strings and numbers, and there are more data types than these. If we need to do some calculations, we have to use numbers, and if we need to do text manipulation, then we use characters, etc. Every data type has its own usage circle and size of bytes inside of the memory when declared. Hence, it is important to use the best data type for the related problem in order to avoid errors and to make your code more readable and maintainable.

1.4 - Bit

A bit is the smallest unit of information inside a computer. It can represent the values *true*, *1*, or *false*, *0*. Several bits can be grouped together to represent other data types. A number of bits that represent a data type is often called the memory allocation for that data type.

1.5 - Byte

A byte is a group of 8 bits that can accessed or modified together. A single memory address often represents the location of a single byte or a start of a group of bytes. Computers often use groups of bytes to represent different types of data. A group of bytes that represent a data type is often called the memory allocation for that data type.

1.6 - Heap

The heap is a location of memory where the program requests the .Net runtime to create new objects. When the runtime detects that the object is no longer being used, the memory it used will be recycled by the runtime for newer objects. This process of automatically recycling memory is called garbage collection.

1.7 - Integer

The integer family of types are one of the most used data types in C# language. The integer represents any number that does not have fractional parts, also known as the whole number (e.g., 1, 5, 27, 13, -145...). An integer can be multiple types, but the one we are mostly using is the Int32 data type. In the C# program, the **Int32** data type is commonly written as *int*. It is 32 bits in-memory size. The *int* variable can be declared, or it can be declared and value-assigned in the same line. The default value for an integer data type is zero (0).

The most common integer types throughout the code are:

1) byte – unsigned integer which is 8 bits represented in memory

2) long – it is 64 bits in-memory signed integer type (*Int64*)

3) short – singed integer type which is 16 bits organized in memory (*Int16*)

8

1.8 - Decimal

Decimal data types in C# represent non-rounded numbers—fractional numbers. There are also few decimal data types that differ by its size in memory, representation, usage, etc. In order to initialize the decimal data type, a **decimal** keyword is used. This type is represented with 128 bits of memory allocation. Another way of saying this is that each instance of this data type consumes 128 bits of memory. For decimal data types, the suffix *-m*, or *–M* must be added at the end of the number so that the compiler knows that it should be treated as a decimal type. If that suffix is not inserted, the compiler will treat that number as the **double** type. *Double* type is the default floating-point type in C#. That means if none of the suffixes are added at the end of the number, that number will be treated as the double data type. It is represented with 64 bits in memory allocation. There is also a **float** data type, whose size in memory is 32 bits. Suffix for float data type representation is *-f*, or *-F* (if not added, then the number will be treated as the double data type because double is the default data type as mentioned earlier).

1.9 - String

The string data type in C# is a type that represents text and works with text variables. In fact, it is an array of characters. Declaring a string data type is done by using the **string** keyword. When a string keyword is used, it means that it is referring to the 'System.String' class (classes will be explained later in the book). There are many extension methods which could be used over some string variable. Some of the most popular are **Concat()**—which combines two strings, **Contains()**—which determines whether the string contains the given string from the parameter as a passed value, **Equals()**—which determines whether two strings have the same value, etc. The default string data type is an empty string. String values from programs will be shown with italics when described in a paragraph like the following: *"This is an example string from a program"*. If the punctuation is outside of the italicized string in this case, it does not exist in the example string value in the example.

1.10 - Boolean

The Boolean data type is regarded as the logical data type in C#. It has only two possible values, and they are **true** or **false.** The Boolean type in code is referred to through the **bool** keyword. The Boolean data type is used very often in programming because it is always required to determine some logical conditions. It is commonly used for comparing things such as number comparison, object comparison, etc. A Boolean is the returned value in every **if** condition in the code (*If-Else* statement will be explained later in the upcoming chapter). The default Boolean data type value is *false*. In C#, the '!' character is used as the not operator which returns the opposite value of a current Boolean value.

1.11 - Var

The *var* data type is introduced in C# 3.0 to implicitly declare variables. So, it can be said that *var* is not a data type; it just represents a way of declaring variables. This means that when some variables with the **var** keyword are declared, we are telling the program that it needs to determine the explicit data type of the variable during the time of compilation. There are also restrictions about the *var* keyword and its usage such that all explicit data types such as **int**, **string**, and **bool** can be class fields.

On the other hand, implicit declaring (*var* keyword) cannot be class fields. This "imaginary" data type can only be used if it is declared and initialized at the same time (value-assigned) because the compiler will adjust its real data type by the value from the right side of the equation mark. A variable declared with the *var* keyword cannot be initialized with the **null** value.

```
var someVariable = "New Text";
var secondVariable = 53;
var thirdVariable; // This will generate a compile error.
var fourthVariable = null; // This will generate a compile error.
```

Declaration and value initialization of the **someVariable** and **secondVariable** is fine because the compiler knows how to determine the data type for these two variables due to the right side of the assignment (The *"New Text"* value has the type of *string* and the value *53* has the type of *int*). An assignment statement is a statement that is centered on a single '=' character where the value or pointer on the right side is set on the variable on the left side. The **thirdVariable** declaring is not allowed because it does not have any initialization of the value. The **fourthVariable** initialization is also not allowed because the compiler does not recognize the type by its right-side value assignment. It is *null*, and *null* stands for referencing the variable pointer to nothing, no object, or no value. In other words, *null* represents the absence of a value, the absence of a number, or a pointer to no object at all, while *0* represents a number between *1* and *-1*. *Double* and *float* types have another unique value known as *NaN (not a number) PositiveInfinity* and *NegativeInfinity*. These unique values are declared as fields on the *float* and *double* number types.

Let's jump into the examples:

```csharp
class Program
{
    static void Main(string[] args)
    {
        Integers();
        Double();
        String();
        Boolean();
        Var();
    }

    private static void Integers()
    {
        int x = 4;
        int y = 3;
        int z = x * x + y * y;
        Console.WriteLine(z);
    }

    private static void Double()
    {
        decimal credit = 170.32m;
        decimal debit = 125.75m;
        decimal balance = credit - debit;
        Console.WriteLine(balance);
    }

    private static void String()
    {
        string firstName = "Tom";
        string lastName = "Holland";
        string fullName = $"{firstName} {lastName}";
        Console.WriteLine(fullName);
    }

    private static void Boolean()
    {
        bool isGrassGreen = true;
        bool isTheOceanRed = false;
        Console.WriteLine($"Is the grass green? {isGrassGreen}");
        Console.WriteLine($"Is the ocean red? {isTheOceanRed}");
    }

    private static void Var()
    {
        var sentence = "Hello World!";
        Console.WriteLine(sentence);
    }
}
```

Here's an example that will demonstrate the data types and help you understand better.

So, here we have a class *Program* with six methods inside of it. The first method is the *Main()* method. This method is called first after we run the program. The only thing that is done in the *Main()* method is to call other methods that demonstrate some basics of working with data types in C#. The first method that is called in the *Main()* method is the *Integers()* method. The *Integers()* method does not have any parameters passed to it. Inside of this method, three integer variables **x**, **y**, and **z**, are declared. The assignment of the *z* variable is the calculation based on the previous two variables which have already been declared.

int z = x * x + y * y;

This assignment does the following calculation: *4 * 4 + 3 * 3*, which equals *25*. So variable *z* is equal to *25*. After this calculation, the program prints the value of the *z* variable to the console line, which is *25*. Keep in mind that the C# compiler will respect the order of operations as programmed in itself and this order of operations is similar to algebra. As the first exercise of researching an aspect of programming on the internet, open up an internet browser and navigate to a search engine (Google, Bing, DuckDuckGo, etc.) and search for "C# order of operations" (without the quotation marks) and click on the first few links that show up in the list. An internet search engine is one of best tools available to a programmer.

After the execution of the *Integers()* method, the program is heading to the execution of the *Double()* method. Here, declaring three decimal variables is done, and these variables are **credit**, **debit**, and **balance**. Variable balance is calculated by subtracting the debit and credit variables. After the calculation, the balance value is *44.57*, which would be printed in the console line.

Now, the next method to be executed is the *String()* method. Here, **firstName** and **lastName** variables are declared, and the program is doing the string manipulation with them to assign a value to the **fullName** variable. By using the interpolation sign '$,' the program is forming the new string, which consists of the *firstName* string value, *lastName* string value, and the space between them. So, the *fullName* variable value assigned is *"Tom Holland"*, and the program prints it into the console line.

Boolean() method is next. Inside this method, two Boolean variables are declared, and what they determine is the following: "is the grass green and is the ocean red?" Again, using interpolation, the program inserts those values into the console line to print these statements. So, the first string which would be printed is *"Is the grass green? True"* and the second string printed would be *"Is the ocean red? False"*.

In the end, the *Var()* method is executed. In this method, the program declares a string data type variable, which is determined at compilation time. During the compilation time, the compiler looks at the right side of the assignment and finds *"Hello World!"* This way, the compiler knows that the sentence variable is of a string data type. After it, the program prints its value on the console line.

Below is the console output of the program previously described.

1.12 - Arrays

An array is a continuous list of objects or values of the same type or super type that has a fixed length that cannot change. In .Net, the array is a built-in generic type of the .Net runtime. The .Net runtime uses the generic array type as a template to create a specific array type. This concrete realization of the generic array type template can only contain objects that are compatible with the specific type that is used to create the specific array type from the generic template.

1.13 - Process

A process is a copy of a program that is actually running in the computer. More than one copy of a program can each run as an independent process simultaneously in a computer.

13

1.14 - Thread

A thread is a single line of execution in a process. A process can have more than one thread running at the same time, and each thread will share all the memory with all the other threads in the same process. Each thread has a thread stack which is used to keep track of temporary variables inside methods. The thread stack also holds the parameters for the methods and records which method to return control to when the currently executing method finishes.

Chapter 2: Branches and Loops

Programming is not always straight-forward. So sometimes, it is all about decisions and conditions. At some point, based on the condition or conditions, the flow of the program could be done in two separate ways. What this means is that if certain conditions are fulfilled, it is required to execute the *A* block of the code, or else the *B* block of the code will be executed. This is called branching. Some code blocks will be executed based on the condition, while others won't be executed at all at the particular point.

Also, sometimes we need to execute some block of the code multiple times and reuse its logic. We can achieve this by looping in C#. The term looping means that a certain code block is executed several times until some conditions are fulfilled. It's all about iterating. Branching and looping in C# depends on Boolean conditions. As mentioned before, based on some Boolean conditions, a certain code block can be executed once or a various number of times.

2.1 - For Loop

In C# programming language, there are several ways to loop over some block of code. The first looping type which will be shown in this book is the **for** loop. *For* loop is used when you know exactly how many times you want to iterate through some block of the code. It is declared with the **for** keyword. *For* loop executes code blocks until the specified condition in the *for* statement returns a **false** Boolean value. The syntax for this iteration is:

```
for (variable initialization; condition; iterating steps)
{
        //body code block
        //execute this code block until the condition is false
}
```

The **variable initialization** is executed only once by the program. It is executed before going into the **body** block of the code inside the *for* statement. Here we are declaring and initializing the variables that will be used inside the body code block. The **condition** part of the syntax represents the Boolean expression on the basis of which it will be decided if it is necessary to re-enter the body code block. The **iterating steps** describe the incrementing or decrementing of some counter. This statement is executed every time after the body block has been executed. We can use the **break** statement if we want to jump out of the iterations in the *for* loop for some particular reason. For example:

```
int counter = 20;
for(int i=0; i<5; i++)
{
    if (counter > 100)
    {
        break;
    }

    counter = 2 * counter;
}
```

Here we have some code block that iterates five times through the body code block. In the code block body, the counter variable is multiplied each time by two. Before this calculation, there is a condition that checks if the counter value exceeds one hundred. It should iterate five times through this block, but if you look closer, you'll notice that it didn't act like that. In the beginning, the counter value is 20. After the first iteration, it became 40, followed by the second, where it changed to 80, then in the third, it became 160, and in the fourth iteration, the condition was fulfilled. So, since the counter is greater than 100, the code exits the loop. Then, it continues the execution of the code below the loop statement. In the *for* loop, there is also one statement which is similar to the **break**, and this keyword is known as **continue**. The *continue* statement means that it is breaking the execution of the current iteration and jumps to the next iteration if the condition is fulfilled. For example:

```
for(int i=0; i<5; i++)
{
    if(i == 3)
    {
        continue;
    }

    Console.WriteLine(i);
}
```

This is an example of a *for* loop. A *for* loop states that a block of code should be executed a number of times before exiting the loop. In the first part of what is inside of the parentheses after the *for* keyword, the variable *i* is declared with *0* being the initial value to control the number of iterations before the for loop completes. In the second part that is after the first semicolon, a Boolean test is defined as *i<5*. This is telling the *for* loop to iterate while the variable *i* is less than *5*. Any test defined for a *for* loop will be executed before the block of code below the *for* loop is potentially executed. The part that instructs the *i* variable to increment by one (*i++*) is found after the second semicolon in the parentheses. After the parentheses, is a block of code surrounded by curly brackets that defines the code to execute in the *for* loop. In this block of code, the

16

variable *i* is tested to see if it has the value *three* and it restarts the *for* loop without executing the remaining code in the loop when it comes across the *continue* statement.

In other words, this part of the program is supposed to iterate five times, and it ought to print the counter number to the console line each time, except in one iteration. This is because of the *if* condition, where the program is checking whether variable *i* counter is equal to three. In the fourth iteration, variable *i* will be equal to three, and the program will execute the *continue* statement, which breaks the fourth iteration from printing number three to the console. However, it does not break the whole loop; it just breaks that iteration and continues the next iteration. In this case, the next iteration is also the last one.

The program output will look like this:

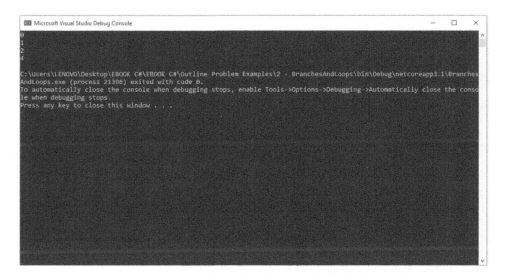

2.2 - While Loop

The next looping statement in C# code that will be analyzed is the **while** loop. This statement also represents the repeated execution of the same code block. The syntax for using the *while* loop statement in C# is shown below:

```
while(boolean expression)
{
        //body code block
        //execute code as long as condition returns true
}
```

17

Code block from the **body** will be executed, while the **expression** variable returns a true value. Unlike the *for* loop, here, the initialization part must be done before the loop itself. Handling of the increment or decrement counters should be done inside the body code block in order to create some logical way of using the *while* statement. Due to the condition of the *while* statement, we may never enter the body code block that is inside the *while* loop. If the condition is false at the beginning, the program will never begin the loop, so the minimum number of iterations can be zero. This cannot happen in a *for* statement because in a *for* loop, the minimum number of iterations is one. Here, the *break* statement could also be made if the program needs to exit the loop due to some reason. In the example below, the condition in the *while loop* is always true, so this loop should iterate an infinite number of times. Though, after the third iteration, the counter variable will equal 270. Since it is greater than 100, this program will enter the *if* block, and it will break the loop, continuing the execution of the code below the *while* statement.

```
int counter = 10;
while(true)
{
    if (counter > 100)
    {
        break;
    }

    counter = 3 * counter;
}
```

The *continue* statement can also be applied to the *while* loop. An example is shown below:

```
int i = 0;
while (i < 5)
{
    if (i == 3)
    {
        i++;
        continue;
    }

    Console.WriteLine(i);
    i++;
}
```

Here, the program is supposed to iterate five times through the *while* loop. In the fourth iteration, when the *i* variable counter is equal to three, the code enters the *if* block, increments the *i* variable counter, and executes the *continue* statement. This prevents the program from doing the console printing of the value three, but rather, it executes

18

the next and last iteration. So, the output of this program looks completely the same as in the example with the *for* loop with *continue* statement above.

There is also a *do-while* loop, which is the same as the generic *while* loop with a small difference. In a *do-while* loop, the body code block executes at least once. The syntax for the *do-while* loop is shown below:

```
do
{
    //body code block
} while (boolean expression);
```

It is important to note that the condition is at the end of the statement, unlike the *while* statement, where it is in the beginning. This makes the code execution of the body block to be executed at least once. The *break* and *continue* statements can also be applied to the *do-while* loop as needed. Here is an example of the *do-while* loop:

```
int i = 0;
do
{
    Console.WriteLine(i);
    i++;
} while (i > 5);
```

At the beginning of this short program, variable *i* is initialized with the value *zero*. Then the program runs a *do-while* loop. The command is that it should execute the body code block while the variable *i* value is greater than five. Now, you are probably wondering how this would print anything at all if the variable *i* equals zero since the beginning, and the condition is—while *i* is greater than five, which is obviously not the case. It is simple: *do-while* will execute at least once, so whatever the *i* variable value is, the first iteration will be executed. Then, after the first iteration, the program will not satisfy the condition, and the looping will stop. The output of this program would be:

2.3 - Recursion

The term "recursion" is typical in programming, as well as in C# programming language. When the problem starts to be too complex, algorithms need to be split into smaller pieces in order to find the solution. Recursion is the programming technique where the program method or procedure calls itself repeatedly to solve that problem. So, to make this easier, recursion is the process of executing a function, which means calling itself inside the body code block function. Some problems which require looping through a particular code block can be simplified and solved with recursion. The best case should be the calculation of the known mathematical problem known as factorial. Factorial of a number represents the multiplication of every number from one to that particular number. The value of the zero factorial and one factorial is one. Below are several examples of factorial notation on the left side of the first or only equal sign. The mathematical factorial symbol, '!', should not be confused with C#'s not operator, '!', which returns the opposite value of the current Boolean value. In C#, the '!' operator always flips a Boolean from true to false or false to true. Remember, the below example is not valid C# code but are examples of mathematical factorial notation.

0! = 1

1! = 1

2! = 1*2 =2

3! = 1*2*3 = 6

4! = 1*2*3*4 = 24

5! = 1*2*3*4*5 = 120

```
static void Main(string[] args)
{
   Console.WriteLine(fact(5));
   Console.WriteLine(factLoop(5));
}

public static int fact(int n)
{
   if (n <= 1) // base case
      return 1;
   else
      return n * fact(n - 1);
}

public static int factLoop(int n)
{
   if (n <= 1) // base case
      return 1;

   int factorialValue = 1;
   int i = 1;
   while(i <= n)
   {
      factorialValue *= i; //factorialValue = factorialValue * i;
      i++;
   }
   return factorialValue;
}
```

In this example, the program contains one **Main()** method, which involves writing two lines in the console. The first line output value is the returned value of **fact**(5) method. While the second line output is the returned value of the **factLoop**(5) method. Both methods have parameters passed inside, and the parameter represents the number that the factorial value program wants to calculate—the *n* variable. Both methods have the checker if the passed number is zero or one because it is the edge case scenario of the factorial calculation *(0! = 1! = 1)*. The second method (*factLoop()*) is the method that is calculating the factorial of the number through the *while* loop. The initial variables are declared at the beginning of the method. These variables are known as the **factorialValue**, which is the return value of the function (inside this variable, the program will calculate the factorial of the particular number). Furthermore, the counter variable *i* represents the conditional controller of how many times the program should iterate through the *while* loop to get the factorial value of a number. In each iteration, we are multiplying the current *factorialValue* variable value with the counter variable *i* and increment the counter by one. After the last iteration, the program will have the factorial value of the passed number, and that number will be returned as a result of the method of execution.

This algorithm could be simplified with the recursion concept. The first method, *fact(5)*, uses the recursion method. The result of this method is the same as the result of a non-recursive method, which was explained above—the solution with a loop. In this method, after the zero or one factorial check, the program returns the passed value that was multiplied by the call of the method with the current context. So, with the *fact(5)* call, the program calculates *5 * fact(5-1)*, then it calls the same method, but with a different parameter passed, this time with the parameter four. The execution of the method calculates the *4 * fact(4-1)*, and this continues until the *fact(1)* is called. The results of these recursive calls are returned, and then used to calculate the factorial of the previous call. The program flow is explained below:

```
public static int fact(int 5)
{
    if (5 <= 1) // base case
        return 1;
    else
        return 5 * fact(5 - 1);   //fact(4) is equal to 24, so this is 5*24=120;
}                                 //check factorial call below

public static int fact(int 4)
{
    if (4 <= 1) // base case
        return 1;
    else
        return 4 * fact(4 - 1);   //fact(3) is equal to 6, so this is 4*6=24;
}                                 //check factorial call below

public static int fact(int 3)
{
    if (3 <= 1) // base case
        return 1;
    else
        return 3 * fact(3 - 1);   //fact(2) is equal to 2, so this is 3*2=6;
}                                 //check factorial call below

public static int fact(int 2)
{
    if (2 <= 1) // base case
        return 1;
    else
        return 2 * fact(2 - 1);   //fact(1) is equal to 1, so this is 2*1=2;
}                                 //check factorial call below

public static int fact(int 1)
{
    if (1 <= 1) // base case
        return 1;                 //fact(1) is equal to 1;
    else
        return n * fact(n - 1);
}
```

You can see from the program output that both the loop and recursive calculations have the same result, which is *120*.

2.4 - If...Else

As mentioned earlier, and as you can see from some of the examples above, the **if-else** statement in C# is used a lot. Conditional programming is required pretty much all of the time. The *if* statement in the program can be *standalone*, or it can also be followed by an *else* statement. The code branching happens in the *if-else* statements. Several choices of the program flow represent the branching term. The *if-else* statements work based on logical conditions, which is, if some conditions are fulfilled, execute this code block, else execute that code block, etc. It is also possible to have nested *if-else* statements inside each other. In the C# programming language, logical conditions from mathematics are supported. Those conditions are:

- Less than: $x < y$
- Less than or equal to: $x <= y$
- Greater than: $x > y$
- Greater than or equal to: $x >= y$
- Equal to: $x == y$
- Not Equal to: $x != y$

There are four specific conditional programming use cases.

The first is the *standalone* **if** statement—if the condition is true, then execute the code block.

The second is the **if-else** statement, if the condition is true, then execute the code block that is inside the *if* part, otherwise execute the code block, which is inside the *else* part.

23

The third type is the **if-else if** statement. This type of statement should be used to specify a new condition to test if the first condition is false.

Finally, the last type is the **switch** statement, which is used if there are many different blocks of the code that could be executed based on some condition.

```
// Example 1: if statement
int exampleOneYear = 1988;
if (exampleOneYear < 1900)
{
    Console.WriteLine("19th Century");
}

// Example 2: if-else statement
int exampleTwoYear = 1988;
if (exampleTwoYear < 2000)
{
    Console.WriteLine("Unknown Century");
}
else
{
    Console.WriteLine("21st Century");
}

// Example 3: if-else if statement
int exampleThreeYear = 2010;
if (exampleThreeYear < 1900)
{
    Console.WriteLine("Unknown Century");
}
else if (exampleThreeYear < 2000)
{
    Console.WriteLine("20th Century");
}
else
{
    Console.WriteLine("21st Century");
}
```

In the first example, in the year *1988*, the condition will not be fulfilled, and the program is not going to enter the *if* code block—nothing will be printed to the console.

In that same year, *1998*, in the second example, the variable year, in this case, is less than *2000*, so the program is going to enter the *if* code block, and it will print **"Unknown Century"** to the console.

In the third example, in the year *2010*, the first condition will not be fulfilled because *2010* is not less than *1900*. The program then enters the else-if condition, and since the year is also not less than *2000*, the program then enters the final *else* branch, which prints **"21st Century"** to the console line.

Now let's transition to the **switch** statement example below:

```
// switch statement
int month = 5;
switch (month)
{
    case 1:
        Console.WriteLine("January");
        break;
    case 2:
        Console.WriteLine("February");
        break;
    case 3:
        Console.WriteLine("March");
        break;
    case 4:
        Console.WriteLine("April");
        break;
    case 5:
        Console.WriteLine("May");
        break;
    case 6:
        Console.WriteLine("June");
        break;
    case 7:
        Console.WriteLine("July");
        break;
    case 8:
        Console.WriteLine("August");
        break;
    case 9:
        Console.WriteLine("September");
        break;
    case 10:
        Console.WriteLine("October");
        break;
    case 11:
        Console.WriteLine("November");
        break;
    case 12:
        Console.WriteLine("December");
        break;
    default:
        Console.WriteLine("None of the months");
        break;
}
```

Here, the program is initializing the month number with value 5. This value indicates the fifth month of the year, which is the month of May. How does the *switch* statement work? It has the *switch* condition in the beginning. Based on that condition, the program will enter one of the cases that are defined below. Every case is something like the *if* statement. If the passed value from the *switch* condition is matched with some case, the program will enter into that code block from that particular case. In a situation whereby there is no matching case for the input, the program will enter the **default** code block. It is also possible not to define the **default** case, but it is preferred to do so because that way, the program will be securing that an error won't happen if there is no corresponding case for the input.

25

In this example, the month value is five, so the program will enter the case 5 code block, and it will print *"May"* on the console.

Let us sum up this chapter with one program that will demonstrate the basics of working with loops, recursion, and branching below:

```csharp
class Program
{
    static void Main(string[] args)
    {
        ForLoop();
        WhileLoop();
        IfElseStatements();
        FibonacciRecursion(0, 1, 1, 10);
    }

    private static void ForLoop()
    {
        for (int index = 0; index < 10; index++)
        {
            Console.WriteLine(index);
        }
    }

    private static void WhileLoop()
    {
        int index = 0;
        while (index < 10)
        {
            Console.WriteLine($"{index++}");
        }
    }

    private static void IfElseStatements()
    {
        for (int index = 0; index < 10; index++)
        {
            if (index % 2 == 0)
            {
                Console.WriteLine($"{index} is even");
            }
            else
            {
                Console.WriteLine($"{index} is odd");
            }
        }
    }

    private static void FibonacciRecursion(int a, int b, int counter, int number)
    {
        Console.WriteLine(a);
        if (counter < number) FibonacciRecursion(b, a+b, counter+1, number);
    }
}
```

In this example, we are exposing the class **Program**, which has five methods inside. The first method is the *Main()* method. This method is executed first after the program is run. The flow of this program is sequentially calling four methods to execute: **ForLoop()**, **WhileLoop()**, **IfElseStatements()**, and **FibonacciRecursion()**. The first one to be executed is the *ForLoop()*. In the body code block of this method, the program contains only one **for** statement. In this statement, the **variable initialization** part contains one variable, which is the integer data type **index** variable. The index is initialized with value zero, and it will be used as a counter in the *for* loop. The **condition** part of this statement is that it should be iterating as long as the index variable value is less than 10. This means that there will be 10 iterations through the *for* body code block. The **step** part in the statement will increment the index variable value by one after each iteration of the loop. Inside the code block of this *for* loop statement, there is a simple line by line output that prints the counter value from each iteration. This counter value is the value of the index variable from each iteration in the loop. The output values will be integer numbers from zero to nine (*0, 1, 2, 3, 4, 5, 6, 7, 8, 9*) in each line, respectively.

After returning from the *ForLoop()* method, next on the line for execution is the **WhileLoop()** method. In this method, the program demonstrates a simple **while** loop statement. At the start of this method, there is the **initialization** part, which prepares for the execution of the *while* loop statement. The integer data type variable **index** is declared and initialized with value zero. This variable represents the **Boolean conditional** part in the *while* statement, and it is also used for the method output to the console. After the starting initialization part, the program starts the *while* loop statement. In the conditional part of the loop, the program says: "While the counter variable index value is less than 10, iterate through the *while* body code block." In the body of the *while* statement, there is, again, a simple output to the console. The program prints the index variable value in each iteration, and also increments it by one each time because of the *index++* statement, which is passed as the parameter of the *Console.WriteLine()* method. As a product of this method, the program will have the same output as in the previous method call (*ForLoop()*). It will print numbers from zero to nine in each line.

The next method to run is the **IfElseStatements()** method. Inside this method, it is demonstrated how the **if-else** statement works while inside a loop. In this case, the program contains one *for* loop statement, and inside its body code block, there is an if-else statement. The *for* loop has its initialization part as always, and also the variable **index** which will be used as a counter as well as the logical part inside this block. The starting value of the *index* variable is zero. If the *index* is less than 10, the iterations through the loop will run after which each iteration *index* will be incremented

27

by one. In the body code block of the loop, there is the core logic. In the conditional of the *if-else* statement, the program checks whether the index variable value modulo two is equal to zero. The '%' sign in the C# programming language represents the modulo mathematical calculation. The modulo operator returns the remainder of one number being divided by another number instead of the quotient, the traditional division result. If the number modulo two is equal to zero, that means that the number is even; otherwise, the number is odd. That is exactly what is coded here. If the index modulo two is equal to zero, the program will print that this particular number is even. If that conditional returns false, the program will print that the *index* variable value is odd. This will occur in ten iterations. So, for every value from zero to nine, the information about whether the current value from the iteration is even or odd number will be printed to the console.

The last method to be called for execution is the **FibonacciRecursion()** method. This method describes an example of working with the recursion principle. The first thing here that should be clear is the Fibonacci sequence. The Fibonacci sequence is a very popular and well-known problem in the programming and mathematical world. It is a sequence of integer numbers in which every element represents the addition of the previous two elements. It is important to say that the Fibonacci sequence starts from the number zero. In conclusion, Fibonacci sequence should look something like this: *0, 1, 1, 2, 3, 5, 8, 13, 21...*

Let us return to explaining the program above. The *FibonacciRecursion()* method has four parameters passed. The first parameter is the current element of the Fibonacci sequence, which will be printed right after the program enters the body code block of the method. The second parameter is the next Fibonacci sequence element that should be printed. The third parameter is the counter variable integer, which controls the number of elements of the Fibonacci sequence that should be printed. The fourth parameter is the total number of elements that the program wants to print out to the console line. This parameter is static, and it never changes its value. In every recursion call, it will have the same value as the value passed from the first recursion call. If there were no third and fourth parameters, this sequence would print the Fibonacci sequence of numbers until infinity. This method is initially called with the following four parameters: *0* for the current element that should be printed, *1* for the next element that should be printed, *1* for step one of the printing, and *10* for the length of the Fibonacci array. In the beginning, the program prints the current element of the Fibonacci array, which is passed as the first parameter.

After that, there is a condition in which the program checks whether the step passed from the third parameter is less than the length of the desired output array. If that condition is fulfilled, the method calls itself again, but with different parameters. In the

28

next call, the first parameter becomes the second parameter from the previous call because, in the previous call, the second parameter was the next element to print. The second parameter, which represents the next element for printing, is calculated by the addition of the current and the next element from the previous call. The third parameter is the step incremented by one, and the fourth parameter stays the same in every call. This way, the Fibonacci sequence is built with the recursion principle of the method calling itself. The flow of the recursion calls are the same as in the recursion subchapter explained earlier. When the last recursive method is being executed, its result is returned to its parent method—the one that executed the child method. In this case, "parent method" refers to the method that has called another method, and "child method" refers to the method that was called by the parent method. The "parent method" is also known as the "calling method," and the "child method" is also known as the "called method." This flow is propagated to the main parent method call. The output of this sequence shall be *0, 1, 1, 2, 3, 5, 8, 13, 21* and *34*, line by line. The complete output of this program looks like this:

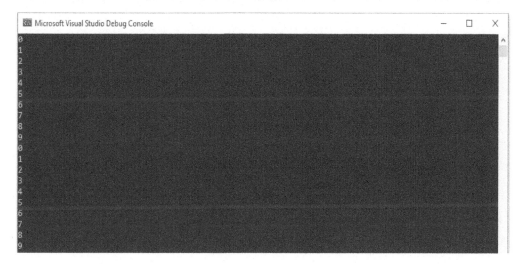

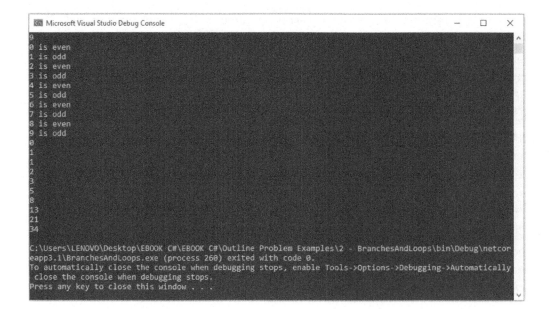

```
9
0 is even
1 is odd
2 is even
3 is odd
4 is even
5 is odd
6 is even
7 is odd
8 is even
9 is odd
0
1
1
2
3
5
8
13
21
34

C:\Users\LENOVO\Desktop\EBOOK C#\EBOOK C#\Outline Problem Examples\2 - BranchesAndLoops\bin\Debug\netcor
eapp3.1\BranchesAndLoops.exe (process 260) exited with code 0.
To automatically close the console when debugging stops, enable Tools->Options->Debugging->Automatically
 close the console when debugging stops.
Press any key to close this window . . .
```

Chapter 3: Methods and Properties

In C# programming language, as well as in the other object-oriented programming languages, there is a term called method. A method is some block of the code which is executed when being called inside the program. It can also be defined as a group of statements, which are supposed to perform meaningful logic. Methods are also known as functions, and they are used to perform certain actions. The biggest advantage of using methods is code reusability. One particular logic can be defined in one place, and it can also be called multiple times in different places in the program. A method is defined with its name, followed by parentheses—**()**. The vital elements of the methods are the access specifier, return type of the method, method name, list of the parameters, and the body of the method. The **access modifier** represents the visibility of a method from another class point of view. There are two types of methods based on the return types; they are **void** methods and **explicit typed** methods. Void methods do not have a return value. They are specified to do some work which does not require returning results. While explicit typed methods are the methods that have the return value. The return types of a method can be various. For example, the return type of a method can be **int**, **string**, **bool**, etc. A method name represents the unique identifier of a method, and it is case sensitive in C#. This means that it recognizes the difference between capital and lowercase letters. For example, *EBook()* method name is not the same as the *EBOOK()* method name. The list of **parameters** is used to receive and pass the data to and from the method. The parameters are elements that are optional inside a method. The parameters can be of any type, and there could be multiple parameters passed. There are a few possible ways of passing the parameters to the method. In a **value** passing method, all changes that are made to this parameter inside a method do not have an effect on the argument which was passed. This happens because the reference of the variable is not passed to the function. It is just a copy of that value. In a **reference** passing method, every change that is made to the parameter has an effect on the argument variable passed. This happens because the reference to the memory location of an argument is copied into the formal parameter. The **body code block** of the method contains a sequence of instructions needed for some logic execution. Methods can also be **overloaded**. Overloading means that multiple methods can be defined with the same name but with different parameters. For example, the compiler won't report an error if the *EBook()* and *EBook(int pageNumber)* methods are defined.

Properties in C# are a mix of a method and variable. It is important to understand the **fields** first. Fields are elements of a class that are used for storing data, and the extension of the field is called property. Reading the data, writing the data to it, or calculating the data is done by using accessors. Accessors in a property are getters and setters. When assigning a value to a property, the *set* is invoked. When using the property value, calling it in some code statement, the *get* is invoked. This way, the program ensures that the reading and writing of data is safe. Let's review an example and introduce this concept better below:

```csharp
using System;

namespace MethodsAndProperties
{
    class Program
    {
        static void Main(string[] args)
        {
            Car car = new Car("Renault Clio");
            Console.WriteLine($"{car.Model}");

            car.Model = "Megane";
            Console.WriteLine($"{car.Model}");
        }
    }

    class Car
    {
        private string _model;

        public Car(string modelName)
        {
            _model = modelName;
        }

        public string Model
        {
            get
            {
                return _model;
            }
            set
            {
                _model = $"Renault {value}";
            }
        }
    }
}
```

In this example, two classes can be seen. The first one is the *Program* class, whose purpose is the same as in the previous examples. Inside this class, there is only one method, and that is the *Main()* method—used for the initial run and showing the actual results of the problem exposed. The other class is the *Car* class. In this class, there are three logical components. The first one is the private **field** *_model*. It is a string data type field in which car model information is stored. Access modifier **private** means that

32

this field data can only be accessed within this particular class. Then, the program contains a **constructor** (which will be fully explained in the next chapter—Classes and Objects). In the constructor, the program is set to define some initial values or states, and this constructor contains one parameter, which is **modelName**, which has the type *string*. In the Car constructor, the program assigns the initial state of the private field *_model*. So, when instantiating the object of the *Car* class, the first thing that is going to happen is the execution of the constructor. There, *_model* field value becomes the value passed from the parameter of the constructor. Every object of the instantiated *Car* class will have this initial value of the private property until something, or someone decides to change it if the class has the possibility to do so. The third component of this class is the *public string* **property** Model. The **Model** property is the public controller of the private field *_model*. Through this property, the program can access the data stored inside the private field. It can also affect its value. This property has both getter and setter. In the **get** part of this property, the program returns the current value of the private field *_model*. The **get** is invoked when the program is trying to "use" the *Model* property. In fact, **get** is invoked when reading the *Model* property inside some statement.

On the other hand, the **set** is invoked when trying to assign the value to the Model property. In the setter of the *Model* property, there is one statement that is assigning one calculated value to the *_model* field. Every time **set** is invoked, *_model* field value is calculated the next way: the static *"Renault"* string is concatenated with the value assigned to the *Model* property. So, if the value assigned to it is *"Talisman"*, the *_model* field would become *"Renault Talisman"*.

In the *Main()* method execution, the program is set to instantiate the object of a *Car* class with the keyword **new**. The variable **car** is created in memory, and it is of a *Car* data type. When instantiated, the parameter passed is a string with the value *"Renault Clio"*. With the creation of this object, the constructor execution is triggered, and *"Renault Clio"* is set to be the default value of the *_model* field. After this, the program prints the current car object *Model* to the standard output. During the process of writing to the console, the **get** of a *Model* property is invoked, and the *"Renault Clio"* value from the private field is read and returned.

The next thing that is executed inside this *Main()* method is the new value assigned to the car Model property. The value that is passed to the setter of a Model property is a string *"Megane"*. The setter then recalculates the new value for the car model (concatenates a string *"Renault "* with the passed string *"Megane"*) and sets *"Renault Megane"* as a new value of a *_model* field of a car object. In the end, the program rewrites the *Car Model* property value to the standard output. This time, the value that is printed is the new value previously calculated, and that is *"Renault Megane"*. The console output looks like this:

3.1 - Access modifiers

Access modifiers are an integral part of object-oriented programming in C#, as well as in other programming languages. Access modifiers are the ones who will determine the level of accessibility of the program components. They define the openness of certain features and try to restrict undesired data manipulation by external classes or programs.

In C#, there are six types of access modifiers: 1) public, 2) private, 3) protected, 4) internal, 5) private protected, and 6) protected internal. The **public** modifier means that the code is accessible from all classes. The **private** modifier defines that the particular code is accessible only from its own class. The **protected** modifier means that the code is accessible within the same class or in a class that is inherited from that class. We will talk about inheritance in later chapters. The **internal** keyword defines that the code is only accessible within its own assembly, and not from another assembly. The **private protected** modifier signifies that access is limited to the containing class or types derived from the containing class within the current assembly. The **protected internal** modifier means that access is limited to any code in the assembly in which it is declared, or from within a derived class in another assembly. The last two modifiers represent the combinations, and they are very specific access modifiers that are used in some advanced programming techniques. If a property, field, or method is declared without an access modifier, it is then recognized as a *private* modifier on classes and

34

structs because the *private* modifier is the default modifier for classes and structs. The *public* modifier is the default modifier for interfaces. From now on, let's focus on public and private modifiers. An example can be seen below:

```
namespace MethodsAndProperties
{
    2 references
    class Numbers
    {
        private int number1;
        public int number2;
    }

    0 references
    class Program
    {
        0 references
        static void Main(string[] args)
        {
            Numbers num = new Numbers();
            num.
        }
    }
}
```

As shown in this example, there are two classes—*Numbers* and *Program*. Inside the *Numbers* class, there are two fields of integer data type defined. The first field is the *number1* variable with a *private* access modifier. The second field is the *number2* variable with *public* access modifier. In the *Main()* method of a *Program* class, we created an object of a *Numbers* class. In the line below that, we can see the offered methods, fields, properties which could be executed over the *num* variable object. You will also notice that there is only a *number2* variable which could be accessed in this particular part of the program. The *number1* variable is not accessible from the *Program* class because it is *private*—it is only accessible from its own class.

3.2 - Return values

As mentioned earlier, methods can have a return value, or they can be *void*, which means that they do not have a returning result. While executing statements inside some methods, the program can run into the return statement. In *void* methods, if the return statement is called, it cannot have the result assigned to the statement. Precisely the return statement may be called in *void* methods, and then the control is passed

35

to the program section from which the call to the void method occurred. Also, the return statement can be omitted in the *void* methods.

On the contrary, typed methods must have a return statement and the value which is being returned. The value returned must be of the same type as the method itself. If not, the compiler would report an error.

To sum up this chapter, an explained program is demonstrated below:

```csharp
using System;

namespace MethodsAndProperties
{
    class Program
    {
        static void Main(string[] args)
        {
            Vault vault = new Vault("qwerty", "Area 51 is real!");

            while (!vault.Unlocked)
            {
                Console.WriteLine("Please enter the access key:");
                var accessKeyAttempt = Console.ReadLine();
                vault.OpenVault(accessKeyAttempt);
                if (!vault.Unlocked)
                {
                    Console.WriteLine($"{vault.GetMessage()}");
                }
            }

            Console.WriteLine($"{vault.GetMessage()}");
        }
    }

    class Vault
    {
        private string _accessKey;
        private string _secretMessage;
        public bool Unlocked { get; private set; } = false;

        public Vault(string accessKey, string secretMessage)
        {
            _accessKey = accessKey;
            _secretMessage = secretMessage;
        }

        public string OpenVault(string accessKey)
        {
            if (_accessKey == accessKey)
            {
                Unlocked = true;
                return _secretMessage;
            }
            return "Invalid access key";
        }

        public string GetMessage()
        {
            if (Unlocked)
            {
                return _secretMessage;
            }
            return "Invalid access key";
        }
    }
}
```

In the following example, there are two classes exposed—the *Program* class and the *Vault* class. The first class explained is the Vault class, along with its members and components. The first things that you will notice are two private fields and one property. The *private* fields are of the string data type, and those are **_accessKey** and **_secretMessage**. The property in this class is the Boolean **Unlocked**. *Unlocked* has a standard getter and a private setter. A *private* setter means that the value of this property can only be assigned inside its own class; in this case, it is assigned in the *Vault* class. So, if someone tries to assign the value to the *Unlocked* property of some *Vault* object inside any other class, the compiler would report an error. This property has its default value set to false.

The next important member of the *Vault* class is its constructor. In the *Vault* constructor, there are two string parameters passed to the body code block— **accessKey** and **secretMessage**. These two values are assigned one after the other to the private fields of this class.

The next component of a *Vault* class is the **OpenVault()** method, which contains one parameter—a string **accessKey**. The body of this method consists of the following: there is a condition check whether the private field *_accessKey* is equal to the value of the parameter passed into the function. If the condition returns *true*, the program sets the boolean value as *true* to the *Unlocked* property of this class. This represents a private set—only from this scope, a value can be assigned to the *Unlocked* property. After *"Unlocking"*, the method returns a *_secretMessage* field value as a result. Otherwise, it returns *"Invalid access key"* to the caller.

The last member of a Vault class is the **GetMessage()** method. The *GetMessage()* method provides *_secretMessage* as the result if the property value *Unlocked* is true; otherwise, it returns *"Invalid access key"*, just like the *OpenVault()* method above.

In the *Program* class, there is a standard *Main* method where we demonstrate the usage of the *Vault* class. In the beginning, we instantiate an object of a *Vault* class named **vault**. At that particular moment, the constructor of a *Vault* class is invoked. Passed values from parameters are *"qwerty"*, which represents the access key, and *"Area 51 is real!"* which represents the secret message. These values are assigned to the private fields *_accessKey* and *_secretMessage*, respectively. Then, there is a *while* statement that executes until the *Unlocked* property of a vault object is equal to true. The logic that is repeating here is next: on the standard output, the program will print a message *"Please enter the access key:"*—requesting the user to enter the access key phrase to unlock the vault. The user's input will be stored in the **accessKeyAttempt** variable. After this, the program calls the *OpenVault()* method of a **vault** object with the *accessKeyAttempt* variable value passed to the function. If the entered access key is not correct, the program will print *"Invalid access key"* to the standard output. This will be repeated until the user enters the correct access key to the console line. After the correct access key has been inserted from the user's side, the **while** statement will abort the looping. Since the Unlocked property is set to true, the secret message will appear on the output as a result of the *GetMessage()* method. The user will be able to see the secret message that was set at the beginning of the program when creating the vault object. That message is *"Area 51 is real!"* The output example is shown below:

You can see that there were two incorrect attempts to unlock the vault. The first attempt was with the *"key"* access key, and the second was with the *"asdfg"* access key. The third attempt was correct, and the secret message appeared in the console.

Chapter 4: Classes, Structs, Enums, and Objects

In C#, every component is associated with classes and objects, and these represent the basic concepts of object-oriented programming. A class is something like a prototype from which the user creates objects. A class represents a single, unique unit with all of its members, attributes, and functionality.

The objects are real-life, in-memory entities. When instantiated, they allocate some memory space and have reference to it. Every object created must be of a class type.

4.1 - Class

As mentioned, classes represent unique programming components inside any object-oriented software. The class is defined with its access modifier, *class* keyword, and a unique name. Inside some class, there could be multiple members such as fields, properties, and methods. The default access modifier of a class is **internal**. This means that if the access modifier is not specified, then that particular class would be treated as **internal**. An example of a class is written below:

```csharp
public class TShirt
{
    private string color;
    public string Color
    {
        get { return color; }
        set { color = value; }
    }

    public TShirt(string color)
    {
        this.color = color;
    }

    public string About()
    {
        return "This t-shirt is " + Color + " color.";
    }
}
```

This class contains its access modifier—*public*, which contains the keyword **class**; it has a unique name: **TShirt**. Inside this class, there are multiple members defined. There is one private field **color**, one public property **Color**, one constructor defined (with one parameter), and one public method **About**.

Apart from the usual classes, there is one special type of class—the **abstract class**. An abstract class is a special type of class in which an object cannot be instantiated. Abstract classes are mostly used to define a base class in the hierarchy, and it is also known as an incomplete class. Abstract classes typically represent a base class. It is designed to have derived classes implementing the abstract definitions. In abstract classes, there could as well be **abstract methods** or non-abstract methods. Abstract methods, as well as every class member that is marked as abstract, must be implemented in the derived class. The classes that are marked with the abstract keyword have the purpose of providing the prototype for the derived classes. An abstract class can have a constructor implemented. An example is provided below:

```
class Program
{
    static void Main(string[] args)
    {
        Animal animal;
        animal = new Elephant();
        animal.LegsNumber();
        animal = new Pigeon();
        animal.LegsNumber();
    }
}

public abstract class Animal
{
    public abstract void LegsNumber();
}
public class Elephant : Animal
{
    public override void LegsNumber()
    {
        Console.WriteLine("Elephant has four legs.");
    }
}
public class Pigeon : Animal
{
    public override void LegsNumber()
    {
        Console.WriteLine("Pigeon has two legs.");
    }
}
```

In the provided example, we can see one abstract class with the name *Animal*. In this class, there is only one member, and that is an abstract void method *LegsNumber()*. When the method is marked as abstract, it means that every class derived from that class, as in this case, an *Animal* class, must have an override implementation of that method. Below the abstract class, there are two more classes, which are the 'normal' classes. Both classes have the override implementation of a *LegsNumber()* method from the *Animal* class. That is because both the *Elephant* and *Pigeon* classes inherit from the *Animal* class. Inheritance will be explained in detail in a later chapter, but for now, the ':' symbol next to the *Elephant* and *Pigeon* class means that they inherit from the Animal class. In this case, this means that they must have their own implementation of the abstract method from the base class. In the *Main()* method of a *Program* class, there is a declaration of an *Animal* type variable named **animal**. Note that there is no instantiation of the *Animal* class because that is not possible, and the reason is that the *Animal* class is an abstract class—so it cannot be instantiated. In the next line, the program is instantiating an object of *Elephant* class into the *Animal* type variable. This is allowed because *Animal* is the base class of the *Elephant* class. After it, there is a call to the *LegsNumber()* method from the animal variable. Furthermore, since the animal is instantiated to be an *Elephant* type, this call executes the *LegsNumber()* method from the *Elephant* class. The next thing is the instantiation of the *Pigeon* object and assigning it to the same *animal* variable. It ends up with calling the *LegsNumber()* method again from the *animal* object. This time implementation of the *LegsNumber()* from the Pigeon class is used. The console output will look like this:

4.2 - Struct

A structure is a custom type where the contents are, customarily, stored directly where the variable is defined instead of the variable being a reference to an object in the heap where the contents are defined. They are declared with the keyword **struct**. They are useful for custom types that act like numbers or for scenarios that need enhanced performance in some cases. Unlike classes, assigning a structure to another variable copies the contents of the structure instead of copying the reference or pointer to the object. This means that the assignment of larger structures will take longer than shorter structures in this case. All structures extend off of *System.ValueType* in C#, including built-in structures like *int*, *long*, etc.

Below is an example of a **struct**:

42

```
struct Point
{
    public int X;
    public int Y;
}
```

In this example a structure or *struct*, **Point**, is being declared with two fields, **X** and **Y**. Both of these fields will be stored directly where the variable that is defined as a *Point* is declared instead of a reference or pointer to an object in the heap. A structure is used to define mathematical-like types, increase performance, and integrate with code outside of the .Net runtime. Remember, a structure cannot be inherited, but it can be boxed. Boxing a structure will be disused later on. A *ref struct* is slightly different than a regular structure; however, this will be left as a research exercise.

A special structure, *System.Nullable<T>*, is used to define a structure that can accept a *null* value which is also called a **nullable struct** or nullable structure. In C#, there is a shortcut to use a nullable structure which is to place a question mark after the structure type. An example of this is *int?*. The .Net runtime has special logic in it to handle this type, especially when boxing and unboxing a nullable structure. It does this in a way that understands and translates between the different *null* values in the .Net runtime.

4.3 - Enum

An **enum** is a special type of structure where predetermined values are named. A type that has a predetermined set of values known at runtime is also known as an enumeration. All enumerations that are declared with the keyword *enum* in C# extend *System.Enum*. *System.Enum* extends *System.ValueType,* which makes an *enum* a structure also.

Below is an example of an *enum*:

```
enum Weekday
{
    Sunday,
    Monday,
    Tuesday,
    Wednesday,
    Thursday,
    Friday,
    Saturday
}
```

A variable that is defined to be this *enum* type may have one of the defined values above. An *enum* type is very useful for values that are known at compile time. In this example, the days of the week are explicitly defined and known at compile time.

An *enum* with the **[Flags]** attribute on it when it is declared is known as a **flags enum**. A variable that is defined to have a flags *enum* can have multiple flags turned on in the variable as defined by the flags *enum*.

The example below shows an *enum* that is defined as a set of flags:

```
[Flags]
enum Quarter
{
    First = 0b_0000_0001,
    Second = 0b_0000_0010,
    Third = 0b_0000_0100,
    Fourth = 0b_0000_1000
}
```

In this example, the quarters of the year are defined as a set of flags. The part '0b' defines the start of a binary string that is represented by a sequence characters '0' and '1'. The character '_' is used between groups of four to make the binary string more readable to the programmer but is ignored by the compiler. An *enum* defined as a set of flags would normally have its fields defined as sequence of increasing values of the power of *2*. Using the method shown in the example above makes creating this sequence easy. The *HasFlag(Enum flag)* method on the *Enum* type makes it easy to test if a specific flag is set. Attributes allow for additional data to be attached to classes, structures, methods, etc., which can be used by the runtime, a library, or custom code to trigger specific logic and/or add extra information. Go ahead and look up on the internet what attributes are and how they are used.

The default base type of an *enum* is *int*; however, this can be overridden. How to override the base type of an *enum* will be left as a research item.

4.4 - Object

Objects in C# represent the real entities in the system, with all of their type characteristics and features. They are located somewhere in memory and have a reference pointer to them. Whenever the keyword **new** is used, an object in memory is created. Objects must be of a specific class type. Every class which is created in C# programming language is derived from the **System.Object** class (inheritance will be explained in later chapters). This means that there is a built-in class Object in C#, and every object of any type is derived from that class. Every object created, besides its own functionalities, also have the methods that are available from their parent class Object. These methods are: *Equals()*, *ToString()*, *GetType()*, and *GetHashCode()*. This can be reviewed in the example below:

44

```
using System;

namespace ClassesAndObjects
{
    0 references
    class Program
    {
        0 references
        static void Main(string[] args)
        {
            var tshirt = new TShirt("blue");
            tshirt.|
        }                    ⊕ About          │ string TShirt.About()
    }                        ⅋ Color
    2 references             ⊕ Equals
    public class TS⊕ GetHashCode
    {                        ⊕ GetType
        private str⊕ ToString
        1 reference
        public stri ⅋  ⊕
        {
            get { return color; }
            set { color = value; }
```

This example uses the class **TShirt**, which was shown in the previous example in Class subchapter. In the Main method, an object of the *TShirt* class type is instantiated. This object is referenced by the **tshirt** variable. In the second line, you can see the available methods and properties that can be executed over the *tshirt* object. Besides **Color** property and the **About()** method that are part of the *TShirt* class, there are also four methods from the parent class Object (*Equals()*, *GetHashCode()*, *GetType()*, *ToString()*).

Each of these methods have a different role in the .Net runtime and can be overridden by the subclasses of *Object,* except for *GetType()*. The *Equals()* method is used to define the logic that detects if an object is equal to another object. The *GetHashCode()* method defines the default hashing algorithm, a method of generating a semi-unique key, for *Dictionary<TKey, TValue>*, *HashSet<T>,* and other collections objects which are used to speed up the logic in these collections. To get the runtime type of any object, use the *GetType()* method. A common use of the result of this method, reflection, will be left as a research item. The next method, *ToString()*, returns the *string* representation of the object. Be careful—the result of this method is not often convertible back to the type of object it came from.

4.5 - Interface

Another important component in object-oriented programming is an **interface**. An interface represents multiple declarations of some functionalities. A class can implement one or more interfaces, but it can only inherit from one class or abstract class. This reveals another C# characteristic—it does not support multiple inheritances. Classes that implement some interface must provide a full definition of all interface

45

members. In the interface usage, there is no manipulation with access modifiers as all the interface members are considered to be *public*. This is because interface existence is all about its functionality to be implemented by other classes. If a class must implement interface members, it means that the interface members must be public in order to be implemented by other classes. The interface is an object-oriented component that has declarations, but it cannot have definitions—implementations. If you try to insert some implementations in the interface, the compile-time error will appear in versions of the C# earlier than version eight of the language. However, in version eight of the C# language, this restriction of not having a default implementation on a method inside of an interface has been removed, but this requires runtime support. A default method implementation in an interface can be overridden by its implementator. The interface can contain properties and methods—everything that can have the implementation. It cannot have fields and a constructor—because it is not a class, and it cannot be instantiated. On implementation of the interface, the class must implement all of the interface members except methods that have a default implementation. However, an abstract class may not have to implement every interface member but can have these unimplemented interface methods as abstract methods. As mentioned, multiple inheritances are not supported in C#, but this can be achieved with interface usage since a class can implement multiple interfaces. An example is shown below:

```
namespace ClassesAndObjects
{
    interface IPerson
    {
        bool IsRunning { get; set; }
        bool IsStanding { get; set; }
        bool IsSitting { get; set; }
    }
}
```

Here we have one interface defined with three Boolean properties inside. A class that will implement this interface must have the definition of all these interface members.

```
namespace ClassesAndObjects
{
    class Person : IPerson
    {
        private string _firstName;
        private string _lastName;

        public Person(string firstName, string lastName)
        {
            _firstName = firstName;
            _lastName = lastName;
        }

        public bool IsRunning { get; set; }
        public bool IsStanding { get; set; }
        public bool IsSitting { get; set; }
    }
}
```

The program contains one class, which is a *Person* class. This class implements the *IPerson* interface that has been declared. This class has two private string fields, which are *_firstName* and *_lastName*. It also has a constructor where those field values are assigned. Besides that, this class has the definition of three members of the *IPerson* interface – the *IsRunning*, *IsStanding*, and *IsSitting* properties. The compiler is fine with this, as there are no errors. But, if we remove any of these three properties from a Person class, the compiler would report an error. For example:

```
IPerson.cs        Program.cs        Person.cs* ⊟ ×
C# ClassesAndObjects                                    ClassesAndObjects.Person                           _firstName
    1     ⊟namespace ClassesAndObjects
    2      {
                  3 references
    3      ⊟    class Person : IPerson
    4          {
    5              private string        interface ClassesAndObjects.IPerson
    6              private string
    7                                    'Person' does not implement interface member 'IPerson.IsRunning'
                  1 reference
    8      ⊟    public Person(s           Show potential fixes (Alt+Enter or Ctrl+.)
    9          {
    10                 _firstName = firstName;
    11                 _lastName = lastName;
    12         }
    13
    14         //public bool IsRunning { get; set; }
                  1 reference
    15         public bool IsStanding { get; set; }
                  1 reference
    16         public bool IsSitting { get; set; }
    17         }
    18    }
    19
```

Here, we have commented out the *IsRunning* property that is inside the *Person* class. A comment starts with *'//'* and goes to the end of the line or starts with *'/*'* and goes to the *'*/'*, and the compiler will ignore comments which are used by programmers to describe or ignore code. The compiler is reporting an error that the Person class does

47

not implement the property, and the program could not build. After this, we will uncomment the property and return to the valid state of a program. Uncommenting is the process of removing the character sequences that defines a comment from the code. Let's create a *Program* class with the *Main()* method inside. From there, we will create an instance of a *Person* class and run the program to check if everything is working well.

```csharp
namespace ClassesAndObjects
{
    class Program
    {
        static void Main(string[] args)
        {
            Person person = new Person("Peter", "Parker");
        }
    }
}
```

Now, we run the program:

Everything went smoothly.

48

Chapter 5: Collections

In C#, there are specialized classes that control data storage and data manipulation. These classes are known as **collection** classes. The collection classes provide support for the most common data structures, such as queues, stacks, lists, and hash tables. Each of these data types will be defined in the following paragraphs. Collection classes have various purposes, but the most important ones are manipulation with a particular data structure. Also, one great purpose is the dynamic memory allocation, which means that when instantiating a collection object, only the reference to that object is created. Memory allocation occurs when you add elements to the collection. So, memory allocation happens on the fly. In comparison, when instantiating an array object of ten integer elements, immediate memory allocation of *10*sizeof(int)* bytes in memory occurs. Some of the collections support this kind of allocation, while some support the super-fast retrieval of an element on an index basis.

Collection classes are split and stored into a few different namespaces. In the *System.Collections.Generic* namespace, there are Generic implementations of some core data structures and some of the main collection classes are defined here. In C#, Generics allows a class to define one or more type parameters for classes and methods. This provide multiple benefits. It prevents other objects, *struct*s, and *enum*s from being inserted in collections in a program where they are not designed to be located. It also gives additional information to the .Net runtime that can allow the runtime to make choices that may improve its performance. A generic class is defined by placing *<T>* after the name of the class when it is declared where *T* is a list of one or more type parameters separated by commas. A generic method is defined by placing the generic type parameter list like above after the name of the method and before the first parentheses before the regular parameter list. An example of this is *Method<T>()*. When a method or class that has a generic type parameter list is being used, the generic parameters must be replaced with real class, *enum*, or *struct* type unless the compiler can infer the type. Generics will be described in more detail later on.

Dictionary<TKey, TValue> is the collection class that stores data based on key-value pairs. It has good data retrieval functionality based on index access. The key represents the index in this class. **List<T>** is the dynamic array, while **Queue<T>** is the collection class that represents the first-in-first-out functionality. Queue data structure means that the first element inserted into the queue will be the first element leaving the queue. If we push three elements into the queue, for example, *1*, *4*, and *7*, and then perform two pop actions, the first pop will take *1* from the queue and return it. Then, the second pop will take *4* from the queue and also return it. After those actions, the queue will be left with only one value, and that is *7*.

Stack<T> collection class represents the stack data structure implementation. It is the last-in-first-out system. For example, if we push four elements to the stack, *1, 4, 7,* and *9*, and then perform two pop actions, the first pop will take and remove the value 9 from the stack while the second pop will take and remove the value *7* from the stack. In the end, the stack will have *1* and *4* values, respectively. These are just some of the collection classes in C#. It would be good to read more about the data structures to enable you to be more familiar with them. A few examples of main data structure manipulation can be seen below:

```csharp
static void Main(string[] args)
{
    //Dictionary
    var colors = new Dictionary<int, string>()
    {
        { 1, "blue" }, { 2, "black" }, { 3, "yellow" }
    };

    Console.WriteLine(colors[1]);
    Console.WriteLine(colors[3]);
    Console.WriteLine();

    //List
    List<int> list = new List<int>();
    list.Add(1);
    list.Add(3);
    list.Add(9);
    Console.WriteLine(list[2]);
    Console.WriteLine();

    //Queue
    var queue = new Queue<int>();
    queue.Enqueue(4);
    queue.Enqueue(3);
    queue.Enqueue(6);

    Console.WriteLine(queue.Dequeue());
    Console.WriteLine(queue.Dequeue());
    Console.WriteLine();

    //Stack
    var stack = new Stack<int>();
    stack.Push(22);
    stack.Push(34);
    stack.Push(11);
    Console.WriteLine(stack.Pop());
    Console.WriteLine(stack.Pop());
}
```

In this example, we have some main actions executed over the core data structures. In this *Main()* method, we have implemented the basic manipulations with the Dictionary, *List<T>, Queue<T>,* and *Stack<T>* classes in C#. The first thing that is instantiated is the

50

dictionary object variable, and it is defined as the int **key** and string **value** pair. In object creation, there are three inserted elements of this dictionary. The first one with key *1* and value *"blue"*, the second one with key *2* and value *"black"*, and the third one with key *3* and value *"yellow"*. These elements are stored in the **colors** object variable. When the program calls the output of the *colors[1]* and *colors[3]*, the *colors[1]* will enter the dictionary and find the value of key *1*. The same will also be executed with the *colors[3]*; it will find the value of key *3*. This will print blue and yellow in each line, respectively. This represents the index-based access to some data.

Next, we have the creation of a list object. This list will contain elements of the *int* type. We are using the **Add()** method to add three integer elements to the list. After that, we generate the output to the console of the third list element. We then access the third element with the index value *2*. In C#, indexing starts from zero, so the first element in any collection is index *0*, the second element is index *1*, etc. Here the output will be number *9*. The following is the *Queue<T>* manipulation. The queue object variable is instantiated, and it is of the *Queue<T>* data type with integer values.

After this, we then use the **Enqueue()** method to insert the elements into the queue. The *Enqueue()* method pushes the values *4*, *3*, and *6* inside the queue.

Then, we use the **Dequeue()** method over the queue variable two times and print each dequeued value. The *Dequeue()* method takes the element from the top of the queue and removes it from the queue. So, in the console, there will be numbers *4* and *3* printed respectively, leaving the number *6* lonely in the queue.

The last one is the **Stack<T>**. This creates the stack object of the Stack data type with the integer elements allowed. After this, we push three elements into the stack, which are the following numbers: *22*, *34*, and *11*.

The **Push()** method inserts the element on the top of the stack. After the push, we then execute two **Pop()** methods and print each value returned from the *Pop()* method. The *Pop()* method grabs the last inserted value and removes it from the stack. So, the output here will be *11* and *34*, respectively, leaving the number *22* alone in the stack. The complete console output looks like this:

```
blue
yellow

9

4
3

11
34
C:\Users\LENOVO\Desktop\EBOOK C#\EBOOK C#\Outline Problem Examples\Collections\bin\Debug\netcoreapp3.1\Collections.exe (
process 3968) exited with code 0.
To automatically close the console when debugging stops, enable Tools->Options->Debugging->Automatically close the conso
le when debugging stops.
Press any key to close this window . . .
```

5.1 - List

The **List<T>** is the collection class that is most frequently used in all collection classes. It is a type whose main characteristic is the element accessibility by index. As mentioned before, the *List<T>* class comes under the *System.Collections.Generic* namespace. The *List<T>* is a class that provides a lot of methods for the list and element manipulation. Some of them are searching, sorting, etc. It is used to create a collection of many different types. It could be a collection of integers, strings, and many more. For the reference types, the list allows null value as an element. It's also possible to insert duplicate values inside any *List<T>* collection. This class can use both the ordering and equality comparer. Arrays are similar to Lists, but Lists are able to resize dynamically, but arrays cannot.

5.2 - Dictionary

The **Dictionary<TKey, TValue>** collection class is, as its name suggests, a collection of key-value pairs. It belongs to the *System.Collections.Generic* namespace in C#. What does *Dictionary<TKey, TValue>* provide? Well, the *Dictionary<TKey, TValue>* class provides something like mapping of related data; it binds the key with its value pair and makes it very easy to access certain data if the key is known. This class is implemented based on the Hash Table data structure. The Hash Table is the data structure that has very good performance on insertion and retrieving data, no matter the size of the data itself. It is especially efficient in searching for data. In a *Dictionary<TKey, TValue>* object, every key must be unique. The key cannot be null, but a key that is a *struct* (except *System.Nullable<T>*) can be a wrapper for an object to get around this restriction.

52

5.3 - ForEach

The *ForEach()* method is an extension method over the *List<T>* class. It is used for iterating through the collection and executing some operations with the elements. In the most common case, it contains code to either read and pass element value to another job or function, or to update an element under certain conditions.

To sum up this chapter, a simple program is written below:

```csharp
class Program
{
    static void Main(string[] args)
    {
        List();
        Dictionary();
    }

    private static void List()
    {
        List<string> sentence = new List<string>()
        {
            "I","am","learning","C#!"
        };

        sentence.ForEach(word =>
        {
            Console.Write($"{word} ");
        });

        Console.WriteLine();
    }

    private static void Dictionary()
    {
        List<string> aWords = new List<string>()
        {
            "apple", "ant", "axe"
        };
        List<string> bWords = new List<string>()
        {
            "banana","bird","ball"
        };
        List<string> cWords = new List<string>()
        {
            "carrot","cat","can"
        };

        Dictionary<string,List<string>> dictionary = new Dictionary<string, List<string>>()
        {
            {"a",aWords},{"b",bWords},{"c",cWords}
        };

        dictionary["b"].ForEach(word =>
        {

            Console.WriteLine($"Words that start with the letter b: {word}");

        });
    }
}
```

Here, we have a class *Program* that contains one method for *List* manipulation and one method for Dictionary manipulation. In the **List()** method, we are creating a List object of strings that contain four elements. These elements are *"I"*, *"am"*, *"learning"*, and *"C#!"* After the variable **sentence** object is instantiated and value-defined, we then execute the **ForEach()** method over that object. This means that we are iterating through the created List and are able to reference the corresponding value in the list by the **word** variable. Here we simply print the value to the console.

The more complex method is the **Dictionary()** method. In this method, we created three new List objects of the string data type. The first list represents the list of words that start with the letter A: **aWords** object. The second list represents the list of words starting with the letter B: **bWords** object. The third represents the list of words starting with the letter C: **cWords** object. Each of these objects is populated with three elements, and three words, sequentially. Then, we have a **Dictionary<string, List<string>>** object instantiation. This dictionary object is a key-value paired object with the **string** data type as a key and **List<string>** data type as a value. This means that a list of strings will be on the value part of the dictionary. This **dictionary** variable object is populated with three key-value pairs. The first one is **"a"—aWords**; and the second is **"b"—bWords**; and the third is **"c"—cWords**.

The last statement in this method is calling the *ForEach()* method over the value of the dictionary variable mapped with the key *"b"*. This means that the program will print to the console a string *"Words that start with the letter b:"* concatenated with each element of the *bWords* list. All of this is demonstrated by calling these two methods in the Main method of the program. The output is shown below:

Chapter 6: Object-Oriented Programming

Object-Oriented Programming (OOP) is the most popular programming paradigm in the world. This paradigm is the successor of procedural programming. Procedural programming represents writing functions and procedures that manipulate some data. On the other hand, object-oriented programming is all about creating objects that have their methods and data all in one. There are many advantages that object-oriented programming has over the procedural paradigm. Object-oriented programming keeps the code much easier to handle and maintain, and it is easier to debug and modify. OOP helps to reduce the amount of time of development, and it also helps build reusable code and components. It is easier to stick to the DRY principle, which tells us that the repetition of code must be kept at a minimum. The DRY principle stands for the Don't Repeat Yourself. Code blocks common to some applications should be extracted and placed in one component from which it becomes reusable and not repetitive. OOP, as its name says, is based on object using and managing. Those objects contain data in different forms. In C#, those forms are fields and properties. It also contains the data manipulation part, which is known as procedures—in C# well-known methods. The objects represent instances of some class, which determine their type. This means that C# is class-based. OOP paradigm allows you to break a problem into smaller pieces—it decomposes it into smaller units, which makes everything easier to handle. Those units are the objects mentioned above. There are four characteristics of the main aspects of object-oriented programming including: **abstraction**, **encapsulation**, **inheritance**, and **polymorphism**. These four features are the laws of the object-oriented programming paradigm.

6.1 - Encapsulation

Encapsulation represents the packing of data into some logical components. It is a mechanism of wrapping the data and binding it into a single unit. Encapsulation is a way of securing the data stored in the classes, preventing access for the components that should not use that particular data. There is a relation between abstraction and encapsulation. The purpose of abstraction is to make certain information visible; the purpose of encapsulation is to select program features that will have a certain level of abstraction. Encapsulation usage prevents and protect the data from corrupted usage, errors, and mistakes. In object-oriented programming, data and its manipulation are almost everything—this is a critical element of a program. If we want to protect certain data, we have to use a *private* access modifier rather than a *public* modifier. If the *private* access modifier is used, the private data is then manipulated indirectly through the properties. This means that the data in a class is hidden from other classes—the well-known data-hiding. As mentioned earlier, this can be achieved by using the private fields and public properties that control the private fields and their values. There are many advantages to using encapsulation, and the reusability of the code is one of them; it makes it easy to change when new requirements are necessary. It is also very good to test the code, such as for unit testing. A simple example of encapsulation is shown below:

```csharp
using System;

namespace Encapsulation
{
    class Program
    {
        static public void Main()
        {
            Person person = new Person();
            person.Name = "Mark";
            person.Age = 21;

            Console.WriteLine("Name: " + person.Name);
            Console.WriteLine("Age: " + person.Age);
        }
    }

    public class Person
    {
        private string _personName;
        private int _personAge;

        public String Name
        {
            get
            {
                return _personName;
            }

            set
            {
                _personName = value;
            }
        }

        public int Age
        {
            get
            {
                return _personAge;
            }

            set
            {
                _personAge = value;
            }
        }
    }
}
```

In this simple example, we show the usage of the encapsulation feature of object-oriented programming. In the *Person* class, there are two fields declared with the *private* access modifier—these are fields that we do not want to expose to everyone throughout the program. These field's values are encapsulated, and available only in their own class. However, we managed to manipulate them indirectly by creating the properties whose task is to control these private field's values. The properties created are the *Name* and the *Age* properties. Both properties have the *get* and *set* accessors. In the *get* accessors, both properties return the corresponding private field value. Similarly, in the *set* accessor, both properties assign the passed value to the private field. This way, we managed to implement encapsulation. In the *Main()* method of a *Program* class, we will test if everything works fine. First, we instantiate the object of a Person class. After this, we set the values for the *Name* and *Age* of that particular object, again using encapsulation because the *set* accessors are called during this operation. Finally, we print the data to the standard output, both *Name* and *Age* of the person, using the *get* accessor in both cases. The output of the program will look like this:

In order to understand this better, an additional example with a bit more complexity is shown below:

```
class Engine
{
    private int _numberOfCylinders;
    public Engine(int numberOfCylinders)
    {
        if (numberOfCylinders != 4 && numberOfCylinders != 6 && numberOfCylinders != 8)
        {
            throw new Exception("Number of Cylinders must be 4,6, or 8");
        }
        _numberOfCylinders = numberOfCylinders;
    }

    public string EngineType()
    {
        if (_numberOfCylinders == 4)
        {
            return "Inline 4";
        }

        if (_numberOfCylinders == 6)
        {
            return "V6";
        }

        if (_numberOfCylinders == 8)
        {
            return "V8";
        } '

        throw new Exception("Invalid number of Cylinders");
    }
}

class Transmission
{
    public bool IsAutomatic { get; }

    public Transmission(bool isAutomatic)
    {
        IsAutomatic = isAutomatic;
    }
}
```

At the beginning of this example, we exposed the two classes at the lowest level. The first class is the **Engine** class. In this class, the first thing that you'll notice is the private field of the integer data type— **_numberOfCylinders**. It is impossible to assign a value to this variable outside of the Engine class because it is private.

The next thing is the *Engine* constructor. The engine constructor takes one parameter— **numberOfCylinders** and that parameter is of the integer data type. Inside the body of the constructor, there is a check to see if the number of cylinders passed is different from four, six, or eight. If this condition is true, the program will throw an exception message that the number of cylinders must be four, six, or eight. An exception in C# is used for handling errors in the program, and all exceptions in C# extend *System.Exception*. For example, if something is detected to be incorrect, then the *Exception* will be **thrown**. That exception should also be **caught** somewhere in the program and inform the user about the error.

59

Throwing an exception causes the exception to bubble up the list of parent methods (or calling methods) until one of them catches the *Exception* and does something with it, which can include rethrowing it. If the top method of the program *Main()* does not catch the exception, the program will end in an error state. An exception that is thrown and not caught in a thread can also cause the program to terminate in an error state. When a program catches an exception, it temporarily or permanently interrupts the normal operation of the *exception* bubbling up the called method chain. A program can catch all exceptions by catching *System.Exception* or one or more specific subtypes of *System.Exception*.

That was a little about exceptions and handling. Let's review the example. If the number of cylinders condition is fine and the code does not enter the *if* block statement, then the private field value is assigned to be equal to the passed parameter. Below the constructor, there is a method *EngineType()*, which is of the string data type. In this method, there are *if* statements that are checking whether the **_numberOfCylinders** is four, six, or eight. If the number of cylinders is equal to four then the *"Inline 4"* string will be returned as the method result; if the number of cylinders is equal to six then the *"V6"* string will be returned; if the number of cylinders is equal to eight, then the *"V8"* string will be returned. If none of these conditions are fulfilled, the program will again throw an exception. This exception will contain a message that the passed value represents an invalid number of cylinders. More details on throwing and catching exceptions will follow latter on.

The second class is the **Transmission** class, and it has one public property of a bool data type that is known as **IsAutomatic**. This property only has a *get* accessor, which means that the value of this property can only be read. The writing into this property (value assignment) is not allowed. What is the purpose of this property if we cannot assign a value to it? Value-assigning to read-only members can only happen as part of the declaration or in the same class constructor. In this case, the value for the **IsAutomatic** property is assigned in a class constructor. The Transmission class has a constructor with a *bool* parameter passed to it. That value is assigned to the **IsAutomatic** property.

Let's move on to the next class. The code is seen below:

```csharp
class Car
{
    public Engine Engine { get; }
    public Transmission Transmission { get; }

    public Car(Engine engine, Transmission transmission)
    {
        Engine = engine;
        Transmission = transmission;
    }
}
```

In this class, named *Car*, we have two public properties. Each of these two properties has only the *get* accessor. This is what makes them read-only properties. As in the *Transmission* class, the value of these properties cannot be directly assigned except in the constructor or on the declaration level. In this case, as in the *Transmission* class, the value is assigned in the constructor. The constructor of the *Car* class takes two parameters, one of the *Engine* data type (or class type), and one of the *Transmission* data type. The two objects passed are assigned to the read-only properties of a *Car* class.

Read-only properties of *Transmission* and *Car* class are encapsulated, nothing can change their value. These values are safe, and there are no worries about something or someone changing the data inside. Let's sum all of this logic application into one unit:

```csharp
class Program
{
    static void Main(string[] args)
    {
        Engine engine = new Engine(6);
        Transmission transmission = new Transmission(false);

        Car car = new Car(engine, transmission);

        Console.WriteLine($"The car's engine type is: {car.Engine.EngineType()}");
        Console.WriteLine($"The car's transmission is automatic:
        {car.Transmission.IsAutomatic}");
    }
}
```

Here is the class *Program* with its well-known *Main()* method. Here, we will manipulate the objects of the previously explained classes and make their characteristics and behavior come to life. The first thing is creating an instance of the *Engine* class with six cylinders. After that, we instantiate an object of a *Transmission* class. This object's property *IsAutomatic* is set to false during the constructor code execution. After we created an instance of the *Engine* class and one instance of the *Transmission* class, we have everything ready to instantiate a *Car* object. A *Car* class requires an *Engine* object and the Transmission object in order to be created. Now, we create an object of a *Car* class with previously successfully instantiated *Engine* and *Transmission* objects as parameters. The program prints the engine type of a Car object. We are able to access this information the next way: first, we access the *Engine* property of a car object. After this information is reached, we can then access the *EngineType()* method over the Engine property of a car class. This method returns the *"V6"* string because that engine is created with six cylinders and is assigned to the car object.

Similarly, this is what we do when reaching the information about the automatic transmission of the car object. First, we access the *Transmission* property of a *Car* object, after this is done, we can then access the *IsAutomatic* property of a Transmission object inside a *Car* object. All of the pieces of information are printed into the console output. The console print looks like this:

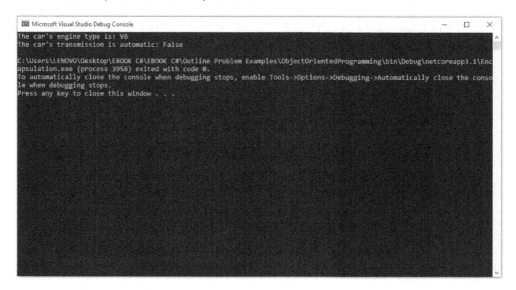

6.2 - Inheritance

Another essential feature of object-oriented programming is **inheritance**. This characteristic is one smart mechanism that allows one class to inherit part of other class components. What this means is that if class *A* inherits from class *B*, the object of class *A* will be able to access the members of *B* class; its fields, properties, methods, etc.

In the inheritance principle, we recognize *Parent* class (the **superclass**) and the *Child* class (the **subclass**). The superclass represents the base class, and its features are to be inherited in a subclass. The class that inherits part of another class is called the subclass. Beyond the fact that this class can access the base class members, it can as well implement its own members and features. The subclass sees all of its features, including that of the parent class features, except those which the superclass specifically marks that it cannot see. The superclass sees only its own features, characteristics, members, etc.

The concept of reusability is completely supported in the inheritance paradigm. The reusability could be mirrored in the example that we need to create some class with some features that already exist in other classes in addition to other new features. In this case, we can reuse the existing feature and just extend that particular class implementation by creating a derived class. We would create a new class with the new features and reuse the existing features by making this newly created class a subclass of an already existing class. To inherit from a class, the symbol ':' is used. For example:

```
class B : A
{
  // code of the B class
}
```
In this example, class *B* is a subclass, and class *A* is the base class. If for some reason, you want to restrict some classes from the inheritance, the **sealed** keyword is used. For example:

```
sealed class Person
{
  // code for the person class
}
class Student : Person
{
  // code for the student class
}
```

This will provide you with a compilation error saying that the *Student* class cannot be derived from the sealed type *Person*.

There is an edge case when the subclass does not inherit from the base class, and that is with the private members of a base class. The subclass cannot inherit from the private members of its parent class. Nevertheless, encapsulation can be used, because if the parent class has public properties with getters and setters that are controlling some private field, then the inheritance could be done over the properties. One important fact is that a parent class can have any number of child classes, but a child class can only have one parent class. This is because multiple inheritances are not supported in C#. However, it can be simulated with the interface usage. In the inheritance paradigm, there is only one member of a class that cannot be inherited, and that is a constructor. The constructor cannot be inherited, but the child class can always invoke the base class constructor code. Please review the example below to obtain a better understanding:

```csharp
class Program
{
    static void Main(string[] args)
    {
        Student student = new Student();
        student.FirstName = "Peter";
        student.LastName = "Parker";
        student.Grade = 98;

        Teacher teacher = new Teacher();
        teacher.FirstName = "Max";
        teacher.LastName = "Weinberg";
        teacher.Salary = 56000;
    }
}

class Person
{
    public string FirstName { get; set; }
    public string LastName { get; set; }
}

class Student:Person
{
    public int Grade { get; set; }
}

class Teacher:Person
{
    public int Salary { get; set; }
}
```

In this example, there is a *Person* class that represents the base class or the superclass. It has two public properties, which are the *FirstName* and *LastName*, and both are the string data type. Now we want to extend this class functionality by creating two more classes, which will be child classes. These two classes are *Student* and *Teacher*. As you can see, they are derived from the *Person* class. The *Student* class has one public property, which is *Grade - int* data type, and the *Teacher* class also has one public property, which is the *Salary - int* data type. The inheritance is set to be proven in the *Main()* method of a *Program* class. First, we created an object of the *Student* data type.

By creating this object, we should be able to access all of the Student class members, as well as the *Person* class members (if they are public). Then, for the student object, we assign values to its own class property *Grade*, as well as its superclass properties *FirstName* and *LastName*. Great, the compiler is not reporting any errors. Let's try to do something similar with the *Teacher* class. First, we created an object of a *Teacher* class; then, we assign a *Salary* property value and the *FirstName*, *LastName* values whose properties belong to the superclass. Now, we run the program and see what happens:

Everything went well, and the inheritance is proven.

It is important to know that there are different types of inheritances: **Single inheritance**—there is only one superclass with just one subclass. See example below:

```
class A
{
  // code for the A class
}
class B : A
{
  // code for the B class
}
```

Multilevel inheritance—there is one class that represents the subclass for one class and a superclass for the other class. See example below:

```
class A
{
  // code for the A class
```

```
}
class B : A
{
 // code for the B class
}
class C : B
{
 // code for the C class
}
```

Hierarchical inheritance—there is one superclass that has more than one child class. See example below:

```
class A
{
 // code for the A class
}
class B : A
{
 // code for the B class
}
class C : A
{
 // code for the C class
}
```

In the inheritance principle, there is one more vital thing to know. It's the use of a **protected** keyword. As promised earlier in the Access modifiers subchapter, the protected keyword will be explained here. The *protected* keyword is used while working with the inheritance paradigm. It is an access modifier that commonly shows up right here in the inheritance feature. A protected member of a particular class specifies the component which is accessible from within the class that it is declared in. Still, it is also accessible from within any subclass of that class. An example is shown below:

```
class ParentClass
{
    private string _privateString = "Private";
    protected string _protectedString = "Protected";
}

class ChildClass : ParentClass
{
    public void Print()
    {
        Console.WriteLine(_protectedString);

        // This statement would not work because _privateString is private field
        // It is accessible only inside its own class ParentClass
        //Console.WriteLine(_privateString);
    }
}

class Program
{
    static void Main(string[] args)
    {
        ChildClass child = new ChildClass();
        child.Print();
    }
}
```

In this example, there is one superclass, which is the *ParentClass* and one subclass, which is the *ChildClass*. In the *ParentClass*, there are two string data type fields. The first field is private, and its value is set to *"Private"*. The second field is the protected field, and its value is set to *"Protected"*. Below the *ParentClass*, there is a *ChildClass* that inherits from the *ParentClass*. In this class, there is only one method—the *Print()* method. What this method does is that it prints out to the console the value of the protected field from the superclass. As you can see, this is allowed, and the compiler did not report any errors.

On the other hand, in the commented code below, there is an attempt to access the private field of a superclass and write its value to the console output. This is not allowed, and the compiler reports an error, which is why it is commented. In the *Program* class, we will demonstrate how all of this works smoothly. In the *Main* method, a *ChildClass* object is instantiated. After this, we then call the *Print()* method over this *ChildClass* object. At that particular moment, the *ChildClass* object state has all the rights to access the protected member of its parent class. That is why this program is executed correctly, and we will see something like this as the standard output:

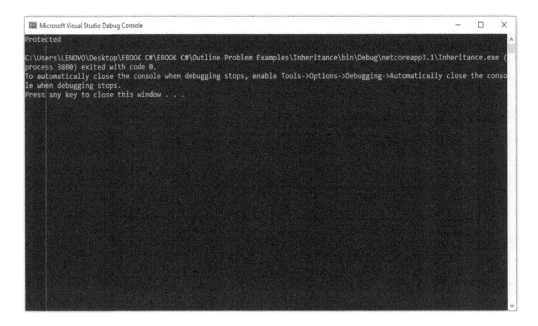

The program has printed the *"Protected"* string into the output, which was expected.

6.3 - Abstraction

Abstraction is an object-oriented programming concept that represents the code implementation hiding or detail hiding. It is related to the encapsulation concept. So, encapsulation represents data hiding, and abstraction provides implementation hiding. One of the advantages of abstraction is reducing the complexity of viewing things such as implementation. Abstraction is a very useful principle because it ensures that only important information is provided to the user. This helps a lot when dealing with security in the application or program. Abstraction can be achieved by using interface components or abstract classes. Let us demonstrate the example of abstraction with the use of an abstract class:

```
abstract class Ball
{
    public abstract string Size();
}

class TableTennisBall : Ball
{
    public override string Size()
    {
        return "Small";
    }
}

class TennisBall : Ball
{
    public override string Size()
    {
        return "Medium";
    }
}

class BasketBall : Ball
{
    public override string Size()
    {
        return "Big";
    }
}
```

In this example, we have one abstract class and three derived classes from that abstract class. The abstract class is the Ball class. Inside this class, there is only one member and this member is the declaration of a public string data type method *Size()*. This method implementation will be provided in the child classes because we want to achieve abstraction. This way, the implementation of the *Size()* method is hidden, which is a characteristic of the abstraction principle. Then, we create three subclasses that inherit from the superclass *Ball*, and these classes are *TableTennisBall*, *TennisBall*, and *BasketBall*. Each child class has its own override implementation of the *Size()* method. *TableTennisBall* class returns a *"Small"* string, *TennisBall* class returns a *"Medium"* string, and *BasketBall* class returns a *"Big"* string as a result of the *Size()* method. Now we get all of this demonstrated in the *Main()* method of a *Program* class:

```
class Program
{
    static void Main(string[] args)
    {
        List<Ball> list = new List<Ball>()
        {
            new TableTennisBall(), new TennisBall(), new BasketBall()
        };

        foreach(var ball in list)
        {
            Console.WriteLine(ball.Size());
        }
    }
}
```

The abstraction demonstration is here. First, we will instantiate a *List* of *Ball* data type objects. Since the *Ball* is an abstract class, it cannot be instantiated, but it can be used as the class type when using the child classes. In this list of *Ball* data types, we have added three objects. For every derived class, we instantiated one object. They all inherit from the Ball class so that they can belong to the list of *Ball* data types. After that, we would want to iterate through the *Ball* list and write the size of each ball to the console. This can be achieved with a *foreach* statement, where we write each result of a *Size()* method called over each object in a list to the standard output. Since there are three objects in a list, there will be three lines of the output. In every iteration, the *Size()* method is called over that particular object. This *Size()* method execution will jump into different implementations each time based on the object type. So, it will return *"Small"* for *TableTennisBall*, *"Medium"* for the *TennisBall*, and *"Big"* for the *BasketBall*. In this way, abstraction is achieved—we have hidden the explicit implementation of the Size() method. The output of this program will look like this:

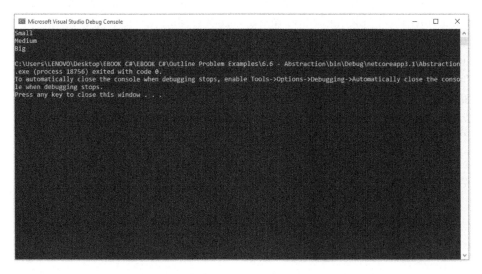

In the second example, we will demonstrate abstraction using the interface components in the program:

70

```
public interface IModernEngine
{
    string EngineType { get; }
}

public interface IModernTransmission
{
    bool IsAutomatic { get; }
}
```

The first thing that we will declare is two interface components. The first interface is the *IModernEngine*—with one string property, which is the *EngineType*. The *EngineType* property has only the *get* accessor, which means that it will be a read-only property in the class or classes that will implement the *IModernEngine* interface. The second interface is *IModernTransmission*. In this interface, there is also just one property. This property is of a *bool* data type, and its name is *IsAutomatic*. This property also has only the *get* accessor—the class or classes that will implement the *IModernTransmission* interface will have a read-only property, *IsAutomatic*, in their implementation. These interface components will serve as a kind of type in this program. Let's move on to the code below:

```
class ModernEngine:IModernEngine
{
    private int _numberOfCylinders { get; }
    public string EngineType { get; }

    public ModernEngine(int numberOfCylinders)
    {
        if (numberOfCylinders == 4)
        {
            EngineType = "Inline 4";
        }else if (numberOfCylinders == 6)
        {
            EngineType = "V6";
        }else if (numberOfCylinders == 8)
        {
            EngineType = "V8";
        }else if (numberOfCylinders == 10)
        {
            EngineType = "V10";
        }
        else if(numberOfCylinders == 12)
        {
            EngineType = "V12";
        }
        else
        {
         throw new Exception("Invalid number of Cylinders, unable to create Engine");
        }

         _numberOfCylinders = numberOfCylinders;
    }
}
```

Here we have a **ModernEngine** class that implements the previously exposed interface **IModernEngine**. It has one private field, **_numberOfCylinders**, and the implementation of the *EngineType* property from the *IModernEngine* interface. This property must have its value set in the constructor because that is the only way besides the initialization on the declaration level. The *ModernEngine* class has one parameter in the constructor, and that is the *int* data type **numberOfCylinders**. In the constructor, there is a number of cylinders check. There are five valid possibilities that will result in the EngineType property assignment. When four cylinders are passed, the property value will be set to *"Inline 4"*. Then, if six cylinders are passed, the property value will be set to *"V6"*.

Similarly, if eight cylinders are passed, the property value will be set to *"V8"*; if ten cylinders are passed, the property value will be set to *"V10"*, and if twelve cylinders are passed, the property value will be set to *"V12"*. If there is no corresponding condition that matches the valid number of cylinders, then an *Exception* will be thrown with the message *"Invalid number of cylinders, unable to create Engine"*. If the property value is set and valid, the private field *_numberOfCylinders* will also be assigned with the passed value.

```
class ModernTransmission:IModernTransmission
{
    public bool IsAutomatic { get; }

    public ModernTransmission(bool isAutomatic)
    {
        IsAutomatic = isAutomatic;
    }
}
```

Here, we created a class that will put the interface *IModernTransmission* to use. The *ModernTransmission* class implements this interface, which means that it contains *IsAutomatic* property implementation. This read-only property is also set in the constructor of the class.

```
class ModernCar
{
    public IModernEngine ModernEngine { get; }
    public IModernTransmission ModernTransmission { get; }
    public ModernCar(IModernTransmission _ModernTransmission, IModernEngine
_ModernEngine)
    {
        ModernEngine = _ModernEngine;
        ModernTransmission = _ModernTransmission;
    }
}
```

In this class implementation, we will start to get more familiar with the abstraction principle. The *ModernCar* class does not implement any of the interfaces. This class contains next members: public property *ModernEngine*, which is of *IModernEngine* data type (as mentioned earlier, the usage of the interfaces in this program is to have a type role), and another public property—*ModernTransmission* that is of the *IModernTransmission* data type. Both properties are read-only because they have only the *get* accessor. We will initialize their values in the constructor of the *ModernCar* class—the main part of this class is the constructor and its implementation. The constructor takes two arguments, one of *IModernEngine* type and the other of *IModernTransmission* type. This means that any object of a class that implements these two interfaces can be passed when creating an instance of a *ModernCar* class. This way, abstraction is visible because there is no explicit type that the *ModernCar* takes as an argument of its constructor. It is not tightly related to some type. Every object of the type (class) that implements these two interfaces can be passed here, and an instance of a *ModernCar* object can be created. In the body code part of a constructor, there is just a property assignment with the objects that are passed when creating an instance of a *ModernCar* class.

```
class ClassicCar
{
    public string EngineType { get; }
    public bool IsAutomatic { get; }

    public ClassicCar(int numberOfCylinders, bool isAutomatic)
    {
        IsAutomatic = isAutomatic;

        if (numberOfCylinders == 4)
        {
            EngineType = "Inline 4";
        }else if (numberOfCylinders == 6)
        {
            EngineType = "V6";
        }else if (numberOfCylinders == 8)
        {
            EngineType = "V8";
        }else if (numberOfCylinders == 10)
        {
            EngineType = "V10";
        }
        else if(numberOfCylinders == 12)
        {
            EngineType = "V12";
        }
        else
        {
            throw new Exception("Invalid number of Cylinders, unable to create Engine");
        }
    }
}
```

Besides the *ModernCar* class, here we exposed a **ClassicCar** class. This class has two public properties: a *string EngineType* and a *bool IsAutomatic*. Again, these properties are just read-only. This class has a classic constructor, with no flexible assignments like that of the ModernCar class. The constructor here, takes two parameters, the integer value **numberOfCylinders** and a *bool* value **isAutomatic**. The *IsAutomatic* property is assigned directly, which is not the case with the *EngineType* property. We have the *if-else* conditions that control the value that will be assigned to the *EngineType* based on the *isAutomatic* parameter passed. The conditions are the same as in some of the previous class constructors (.."V6", "V8", "V10"..). There is also an exceptional situation if there is no corresponding condition for property assignment.

Now, let's bring all of this together and demonstrate the use of interfaces and what they bring here.

```
class Program
{
    static void Main(string[] args)
    {
        ClassicCar classicCar = new ClassicCar(6, true);
        Console.WriteLine(classicCar.EngineType);

        ModernTransmission modernTransmission = new ModernTransmission(true);
        ModernEngine modernEngine = new ModernEngine(6);
        ModernCar modernCar = new ModernCar(modernTransmission, modernEngine);
        Console.WriteLine(modernCar.ModernEngine.EngineType);
    }
}
```

A standard *Main* function inside the *Program* class brings us the following logic this time: The first thing here is the creation of the *ClassicCar* object instance. The *ClassicCar* constructor is invoked with the six cylinders and a true value for *IsAutomatic* property. The *EngineType* property assigned to this object is *"V6"* because of the parameter passed while creating an instance of the *ClassicCar* object. After this, we print the *EngineType* of the previously created object to the console output. "V6" should be seen on the screen.

The work with the *ClassicCar* class is finished, we are now moving to the *ModernCar* class, which is of much more interest to us at this moment. We are now going to create a *ModernTransmission* object. This object is created with the true value passed to the constructor. This results in a true value assignment to the *IsAutomatic* property of the *ModernTransmission* object that is created. Since the *ModernTransmission* class implements the *IModernTransmission* interface, it can be assumed that the **modernTransmission** variable is of the *IModernTransmission* type.

Next, the *ModernEngine* object is created with the six cylinders assigned to its *EngineType* property—"V6". For this object, we can apply a similar logical conclusion regarding the *ModernTransmission* object. So, the created object variable **modernEngine** can be assumed that it is of the *IModernEngine* type. This is because the *ModernEngine* class implements the *IModernEngine* interface. Now, everything is prepared for creating a *ModernCar* object. The *ModernCar* object requires an object of an *IModernTransmission* type and the object of an *IModernEngine* type in order to be instantiated.

Let's now create a *ModernCar* object. We will be doing this by passing the **modernTransmission** object and the **modernEngine** object to the instance creation. This invokes the constructor of a *ModernCar* class. The two passed objects are then assigned to the public properties of a *ModernCar* class, and the **modernCar** variable object is created. In the end, we then print the **modernCar** engine type to the console— this is done by accessing the *ModernEngine* property, and accessing the *EngineType* property of a *ModernEngine* property. The value that should be printed is "V6" just like in the case of the classic car object. The output of this program is seen below:

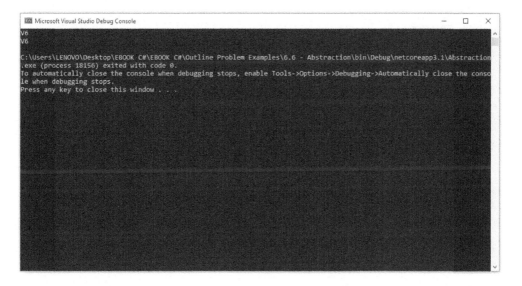

6.4 - Polymorphism

Polymorphism is an object-oriented programming paradigm that stands for the usage of something with multiple forms. What this means is that one property or a function with the same name can have multiple different functionalities—implementations. In fact, the ability of a class to have multiple functionalities with the same name is Polymorphism. It is the fourth and probably the core paradigm in object-oriented programming concepts. Polymorphism happens when multiple classes are related to each other and are all connected by the inheritance principle. Inheritance and Polymorphism are tightly coupled; they go together in most cases. Inheritance enables fields, properties, and methods inheritance of the other classes, and the Polymorphism is there to use these members in order to perform different jobs. This allows programmers to execute a single action in a few different ways. Polymorphism can be static or dynamic. Static Polymorphism is also known as the compile-time Polymorphism, and Dynamic Polymorphism is called the runtime polymorphism. Static Polymorphism happens in the compile-time, while that of dynamic happens in the runtime. Static Polymorphism is when the compiler chooses which overloaded method to call based on the type(s) of the parameters that is attempted to be used in the method call and the available overloaded methods. The example of the compile-time Polymorphism is given below:

```
using System;

namespace Polymorphism
{
    class Program
    {
        static void Main(string[] args)
        {
            Printer printer = new Printer();
            printer.PrintData("New Text");
            printer.PrintData(10);
            printer.PrintData(10.43);
        }
    }

    class Printer
    {
        public void PrintData(string text)
        {
            Console.WriteLine(text);
        }

        public void PrintData(int number)
        {
            Console.WriteLine(number);
        }

        public void PrintData(double decimalNumber)
        {
            Console.WriteLine(decimalNumber);
        }
    }
}
```

In this example, there is a *Printer* class that contains three methods. Each of these methods have the same name—*PrintData()*. The only difference between them is the parameter. The first method takes a string data type parameter; the second takes an *int* data type parameter, and the last method takes a double data type parameter. Each method does the same job—it prints the value of the passed parameter to the console output. How does the compiler allow us to create three methods with the same name? Well, this was mentioned in previous chapters. The compiler won't let you create multiple methods with the same name and with the same parameter types in that same order. The uniqueness of the method is not just its name; it also includes its parameters—the whole method **signature**. The thing you see here is called method overloading, which was explained in some of the previous chapters. Overloading represents polymorphism in compile-time. In this case, the same method name, but different implementation. In the *Program* class, the *Main()* method contains an instantiation of the Printer class. The **printer** object then calls the *PrintData()* method three times, each time with the different parameter type. The first call is with the string argument passed, the second is with the *int* argument passed, and the third is with the double argument passed. Based on the parameter type, the program will recognize the method of implementation it should enter in the *Printer* class. This program has the output that can be seen below:

The second type of polymorphism is dynamic polymorphism, which happens in runtime. An example of dynamic polymorphism is given below:

```csharp
class Vehicle
{
    public bool IsAutomatic { get; }

    public Vehicle(bool _IsAutomatic)
    {
        IsAutomatic = _IsAutomatic;
    }
}

class Car : Vehicle
{
    public int TrunkCapacity { get; }

    public Car(int _TruckCapacity, bool _IsAutomatic) : base(_IsAutomatic)
    {
        TrunkCapacity = _TruckCapacity;
    }
}

class Truck : Vehicle
{
    public int BedCapacity { get; }

    public Truck(int _BedCapacity, bool _IsAutomatic) : base(_IsAutomatic)
    {
        BedCapacity = _BedCapacity;
    }
}
```

Here we have one base class whose name is **Vehicle**. This class has a public read-only property whose name is **IsAutomatic**. In the constructor, you will notice that we only assigned the value to this property. Below the *Vehicle* class, there are two more classes whose role is to serve as the child classes of a *Vehicle*. The first subclass is a **Car** class. It inherits from a base class, and also contains one property of its own. This property is called *TrunkCapacity*, and it is also a read-only property. The *Car* class contains the constructor, which takes two arguments; the *_TrunkCapacity*, and *bool* value *_IsAutomatic*. Note here that besides the normal constructor inscription, there is a **:base(_IsAutomatic)** suffix to it. The **base** keyword signifies that the superclass constructor should also be invoked, then we pass the *_IsAutomatic* parameter to it. This way, the object of the Car class will set the initial value of its superclass read-only property **IsAutomatic**. The **_TrunkCapacity** parameter is normally assigned to the *TrunkCapacity* property of the *Car* class in the body code part of its own constructor. The **Truck** class also inherits from the *Vehicle* class and has the same functional logic as the *Car* class. This class also has one personal read-only property *BedCapacity* and a constructor of its own. The constructor works in the same principle as the *Car* class. It takes two arguments, **_BedCapacity** and **_IsAutomatic** *bool* value. The base constructor is also invoked by passing the *_IsAutomatic* value to it, and the *BedCapacity* is normally assigned in the *Truck()* constructor. Let's put this all to work in the *Main()* method of a *Program* class.

```
class Program
{
    static void Main(string[] args)
    {
        Car car = new Car(1000, true);
        Truck truck = new Truck(3000, false);

        Console.WriteLine($"Car trunk capacity: {car.TrunkCapacity}");
        Console.WriteLine($"Truck bed capacity: {truck.BedCapacity}");
    }
}
```

First, we created a *Car* object by passing *1000* to the car trunk capacity and a *true* value for the information about whether the car is automatic. After this, we create a *Truck* object by passing *3000* to the truck bed capacity and a *false* value for the information about whether the truck is automatic. After the objects were instantiated, we then printed the trunk capacity of the car and the bed capacity of the truck, line by line. The output of this program was as follows:

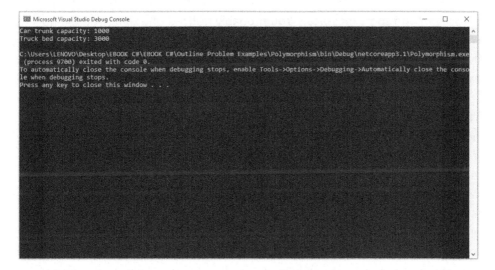

Another example of dynamic polymorphism is the following:

```csharp
class Sport   // Base class (parent)
{
    public virtual void Info()
    {
        Console.WriteLine("The Sport message.");
    }
}

class Football : Sport   // Derived class (child)
{
    public override void Info()
    {
        Console.WriteLine("The best sport is football.");
    }
}

class Basketball : Sport   // Derived class (child)
{
    public override void Info()
    {
        Console.WriteLine("The best sport is basketball");
    }
}
```

In this example, we have one class that acts as a superclass—the **Sport** class. Inside that class, there is one void method **Info()**, that does the printing to the output. A simple print of the message: "The sport message." You probably noticed one thing you did not see until now—the **virtual** keyword. The virtual method represents a method that could be redefined in the child classes. The implementation of a virtual method exists in the superclass as well as in the derived classes. It is used when we have a default functionality, and when we want to extend or change that functionality in the child class. This virtual method can be overridden in the subclass, but it is created and initially defined in the superclass. These steps are next: first, create a virtual method—mark it with the *virtual* keyword in the base class, and then override that method implementation in the derived classes using the override keyword. It is obvious that when a method in the derived class has the same implementation as in the base class, it is not necessary to override it. When called, the program will jump to the base class implementation of the method. In conclusion, overriding the virtual method in the derived classes is optional. Unlike in the abstract methods, where you must override and implement the method. The overridden method provides a new and different implementation, which is the best example of polymorphism. It is important to say that we cannot override non-virtual methods. All of the methods in C# are non-virtual by default. Let's go back to the example. So, in our base class, we have one virtual method which can be overridden in the derived classes. Besides the base class Sport, there are two other derived classes—*Football* and *Basketball*. The *Football* class overrides the *Info()* method from the parent class and writes the *"The best sport is football"*. message to the console output. The Basketball class also overrides the *Info()* method from the

80

parent class and writes the *"The best sport is basketball"* message to the console output. Let's see how all this works together in one method:

```
class Program
{
    static void Main(string[] args)
    {
        Sport sport = new Sport();
        Sport football = new Football();
        Sport basketball = new Basketball();

        sport.Info();
        football.Info();
        basketball.Info();
    }
}
```

Here's our well-recognizable *Main()* method inside the *Program* class. We instantiate three objects at the beginning, all three of the *Sport* class type. The first one is instantiated as the base class object *Sport*. The second object is instantiated as *Football*, and the third object is instantiated as a *Basketball* object. Remember that all three objects belong to the *Sport* class type. *Sport* belongs to the *Sport* class type because it is the core class, while *Football* and *Basketball* also belong to the Sport class type because they inherit from the *Sport* class. After the objects are created, we can execute some functionality over them. First, we run the *Info()* method over the core sports object, then we run the *Info()* method over the football object, and lastly, we run the *Info()* method over the basketball object. The first call will jump into the virtual method implementation in the base class, the second will jump into the *Football* class overridden method, and the third call will execute the *Basketball* class overridden method. It will all result in the next output:

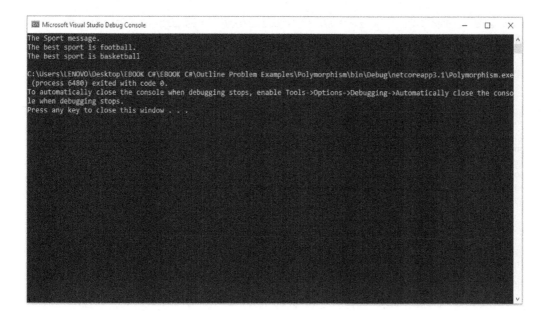

Chapter 7: SOLID Principles

SOLID principles represent strategies programmers should follow while programming in C#. The first five object-oriented design principles are SOLID design. When following these principles combined, they make everything easier while coding. They make it easy to develop applications, or any kind of software that is easily susceptible to changes. If the programmer or the team follows these principles, maintaining, and extending the code will be far more comfortable.

Following SOLID principles makes developers avoid poor coding practices, and makes the system comfortable for refactoring. SOLID makes the software suitable for adaptive and agile development. If coding is not completed with a SOLID design, every small request for a change in the code might become very stressful and painful for a developer. If the application design and architecture are going in the wrong direction, every change, even the smallest, could cause significant problems and large changes in the particular software. That is not ideal. Changes and new features are part of software development, they will always exist, and they are not to be blamed.

A common mistake that has been made over the course of development is adding more responsibilities to a class that are not suited for that. It is bad to add more functionality that is not related to a certain class. Also, when developers force the classes to depend on each other, at some point, a change in one class will affect the other class also. So, making the classes and components tightly coupled is a journey to failure. Duplicating code throughout an application should also be bypassed. These are just some of the mistakes that are slipping through a developer's hands. The solution to all of these potential problems is choosing the right architecture of the application from the start, following design principles throughout development, and choosing the correct design patterns in order to produce software based on its terms.

What you should also know are different design patterns and what they represent. Design patterns represent a general solution to the most commonly repeated problem in software development design. It is a template of how to solve some obstacles. So, it does not represent finished code that you can implement into your software—it is just a description of how you should do it. The best practices that are adapted by experienced software developers are design patterns. Every design pattern defines the problem, the solution, the moment of applying the solution, and its potential outcomes. Each of them gives you some implementation examples and hints on how to achieve them. It would be good if you could read more about design patterns and try to implement them on your own for better understanding. For now, let's return to the SOLID principles.

There are five principles included in this paradigm. Each of them represents a letter in the SOLID term. **S** stands for the Single Responsibility Principle (SRP), **O** stands for Open-Closed Principle (OCP), **L** stands for Liskov Substitution Principle (LSP), **I** stands for the Interface Segregation principle (ISP), and **D** stands for Dependency Inversion Principle (DIP).

7.1 - Single Responsibility Principle

The Single Responsibility Principle says, "Every software module should have only one reason to change." What this means is that every software module, structure, class, and component in the application should only have one job to do. Every little thing in that module should just have one purpose. This means that a particular software component should not contain multiple responsibilities in it. It should serve only one duty. It does not mean that the software modules you are building should only have one property or one method. There could be as many members as needed as long as they serve a single responsibility. This principle provides us with the best way of recognizing classes at the start of the prototype phase of a software product. It makes you think of all the directions some software modules can change. Only when there is a clear understanding of how software should work can the best separation of responsibilities be achieved. Let's look at examples:

```csharp
using System;
using System.Diagnostics;

namespace SingleResponsibilityPrinciple
{
    class Program
    {
        static void Main(string[] args)
        {
            Engine engine = new Engine(8);
            Transmission transmission = new Transmission(true);
            Car car = new Car(transmission,engine);

            Debug.WriteLine($"The car has a {car.Engine.EngineType}");
        }
    }

    class Car
    {
        public Engine Engine { get; }
        public Transmission Transmission { get; }
        public Car(Transmission _Transmission, Engine _Engine)
        {
            Engine = _Engine;
            Transmission = _Transmission;
        }
    }
```

```csharp
class Engine
{
    private int _numberOfCylinders { get; }
    public string EngineType { get; }
    public Engine(int numberOfCylinders)
    {
        if (numberOfCylinders == 4)
        {
            EngineType = "Inline 4";
        }
        else if (numberOfCylinders == 6)
        {
            EngineType = "V6";
        }
        else if (numberOfCylinders == 8)
        {
            EngineType = "V8";
        }
        else if (numberOfCylinders == 10)
        {
            EngineType = "V10";
        }
        else if(numberOfCylinders == 12)
        {
            EngineType = "V12";
        }
        else
        {
            throw new Exception("Invalid number of Cylinders, unable to create Engine");
        }

        _numberOfCylinders = numberOfCylinders;
    }
}

class Transmission
{
    public bool IsAutomatic { get; }
    public Transmission(bool isAutomatic)
    {
        IsAutomatic = isAutomatic;
    }
}
}
```

In this small, but very clear software module, we have a clear design provided. There are three classes that provide distinct responsibilities. *Car*, *Engine*, and *Transmission* classes are the classes that obviously represent one responsibility. They all serve the car with mechanical object detailing. *Engine* and *Transmission* are the *Car* "parts," and the car object is made of the *Engine* and *Transmission* object. In this module, there are no different types of behavior and logic. Each part is about car detail functioning. The *Program* class just puts all of these classes together in one functioning module and representation. In the *Main()* method, there is, first, the creation of the submodules, which are the *Engine* and *Transmission* objects. After this, an instance of the *Car* is

85

created using those previously created objects. In the end, there is a print of the car engine type information onto the debugging console.

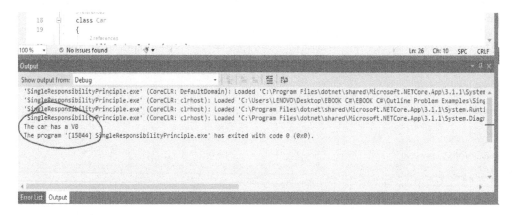

Let's review the second example:

```csharp
public class Worker
{
    public int WorkerId { get; set; }
    public string WorkerName { get; set; }

    public bool InsertWorkerToDB(Worker worker)
    {
        // Insert into db table.
        return true;
    }

    public bool RemoveWorkerFromDB(Worker worker)
    {
        // Delete from db table.
        return true;
    }

    public void GenerateWorkerInformationDocumentPDF(Worker worker)
    {
        // Generate document
    }
}
```

In this example, you can clearly see one class *Worker*. The *Worker* class has three methods inside, and as you can see, this class does not serve one responsibility. There are methods for database actions, and there is one method that has nothing to do with the previous responsibility. The third method is responsible for creating a document that prints information about some workers. This class does not follow a single responsibility principle, so let us refactor this code to get the SRP on the way.

```
public class Worker
{
    public int WorkerId { get; set; }
    public string WorkerName { get; set; }

    public bool InsertWorkerToDB(Worker worker)
    {
        // Insert into db table.
        return true;
    }

    public bool RemoveWorkerFromDB(Worker worker)
    {
        // Delete from db table.
        return true;
    }
}

public class Reports
{
    public void GenerateWorkerInformationDocumentPDF(Worker worker)
    {
        // Generate document
    }
}
```

Now, this is better. Here we split the logic into two classes. One class is for the execution of the database actions, creating and deleting the worker entity. The *Worker* class now serves only one responsibility, and that is handling the database actions. The second class, which is known as the *Reports* class, is created to handle the reporting and documents section. We moved the document generating method to this class, and now everything looks perfect. Maybe tomorrow, the client will ask us to generate some more types of documents. In that case, all of the new methods related to the documents and reports will be in the *Reports* class. For example, if the client asks us to produce functionality for generating a word document with all the *Worker* information in it. Below the PDF creation method, we would implement the *WORD()* creation method, and everything will stay according to the single responsibility principle.

7.2 - Open-Closed Principle

The definition of the Open-Close principle is that the software modules, classes, and components, should be open for extension, but closed for modification. This principle says that any software module should easily be able to extend its functionality without changing the core implementations that already exist. Any application or software module should be flexible and adaptable to changes. Every software requires changes many times through the development cycle; that is why every modification should always be double-checked before completing it. The open-closed principle states that the current behavior of the application or feature can perpetually be extended without having to transform its present implementation. So, new features should be implemented by writing the new code and leaving the existing code as it is. This is because if we change the current implementation, we may make a bug in the current feature, which was previously stated as the good working one. Following the open-closed principle, we can reduce the risk of crashing the present implementation of some features. Also, it is desirable to have every method and feature unit-tested, so that if we change the existing implementation somewhere, it is also often needed to change the unit test, and this extends the development time. Inheritance is always something that leads us to fulfill the open-closed principle. If this sounds good, let's review examples:

```csharp
using System;

namespace OpenClosedPrinciple
{
    class Program
    {
        static void Main(string[] args)
        {
            Car car = new Car(1000, true);
            Truck truck = new Truck(3000, false);

            Console.WriteLine($"Car trunk capacity: {car.TrunkCapacity}");
            Console.WriteLine($"Truck bed capacity: {truck.BedCapacity}");
        }
    }

    class Car:Vehicle
    {
        public int TrunkCapacity { get; }

        public Car(int _TruckCapacity, bool _IsAutomatic):base(_IsAutomatic)
        {
            TrunkCapacity = _TruckCapacity;
        }
    }

    class Truck:Vehicle
    {
        public int BedCapacity { get; }

        public Truck(int _BedCapacity, bool _IsAutomatic):base(_IsAutomatic)
        {
            BedCapacity = _BedCapacity;
        }
    }

    class Vehicle
    {
        public bool IsAutomatic { get; }

        public Vehicle(bool _IsAutomatic)
        {
            IsAutomatic = _IsAutomatic;
        }
    }
}
```

In this example, we have three classes of interest. One is the superclass *Vehicle*, and the other two, *Truck* and *Car* are the derived classes. In the superclass, there is one property that is of big interest here. This property, called *IsAutomatic*, could be used by the objects of the derived classes, as well as in the core class—the superclass. With further implementation, while the lines of code are getting bigger and bigger, there is a big potential to have many references to this property because it could be used by three class objects (*Vehicle, Car, Truck*). If there is a need for some modification in the derived classes, it would be fine to add properties and methods to describe those objects further. This means that they are opened to the extension. However, if there is a need for changing anything about the *IsAutomatic* property, it would create a big mess, and refactoring through every reference to that property should be done. So, as you can see, that would not be such a smart idea. The open-closed principle is reflected in this property. This property is closed for modification because it could potentially lead to enormous refactoring. Instead of changing the *IsAutomatic* property in the superclass, the new property should be added to the superclass, and the derived class constructors should be extended. This actually depends on what you are trying to accomplish. Maybe you want to extend only one derived class; in that case, you would add one property only in its child class.

Let's introduce another example...

Let us assume that a company has employees—software engineers—and the director needs a program to calculate the total cost of all the salaries he needs to pay to employees. That's easy—the implementation could be like this:

```
public class SoftwareEngineerSalary
{
    public double Coefficient { get; set; }
    public double SkillFactor { get; set; }
}

public class TotalSalaryCost
{
    public double TotalSalary(SoftwareEngineerSalary[] salaries)
    {
        double cost = 0;
        foreach (var salary in salaries)
        {
            cost += salary.Coefficient * 1000 + salary.SkillFactor;
        }
        return cost;
    }
}
```

This looks great, and it works correctly. For now, there are no issues, and the program does not violate the single responsibility principle. But the company has different types of employees, and they all receive different salaries. We did not think about that. The information given is that there are two types of employees—the software engineers and the QA engineers; their salaries are calculated differently, so we would need to implement that case. This won't be a problem though, as we can use the code below:

```csharp
public class SoftwareEngineerSalary
{
    public double Coefficient { get; set; }
    public double SkillFactor { get; set; }
}

public class QAEngineerSalary
{
    public double NumberOfHours { get; set; }
}

public class TotalSalaryCost
{
    public double TotalSalary(object[] salaries)
    {
        double cost = 0;
        SoftwareEngineerSalary softwareEngineerSalary;
        QAEngineerSalary qaEngineerSalary;
        foreach (var salary in salaries)
        {
            if(salary is SoftwareEngineerSalary)
            {
                softwareEngineerSalary = (SoftwareEngineerSalary)salary;
                cost += softwareEngineerSalary.Coefficient * 1000 +
softwareEngineerSalary.SkillFactor;
            }
            else if(salary is QAEngineerSalary)
            {
                qaEngineerSalary = (QAEngineerSalary)salary;
                cost += qaEngineerSalary.NumberOfHours * 700;
            }
        }
        return cost;
    }
}
```

We are done with the changes here. We have managed to introduce the QA engineer salary calculation into the program. Now we can also add a Manager salary calculation here. That can be done by adding another *if* block into the *TotalSalary()* method of the *TotalSalaryCost* class. But there is one big problem here. Every time we add a new position and its calculation formula for the salary, we also need to alter the *TotalSalary()* method implementation. So, this means that the *TotalSalaryCost* class is not closed for modification, and we must modify it every time we get a request for a change. How can we implement this better to avoid this situation? Generally, we can introduce the abstractions; we could implement this by using the interfaces or abstract classes and decouple the tight relations in the concrete class code. It would make every new request easier to handle without changing the core calculation method. Let us choose the abstract class component in order to solve this situation in the best way possible. The final solution would be:

```csharp
public abstract class Salary
{
    public abstract double TotalSalaryCost();
}
public class SoftwareEngineerSalary : Salary
{
    public double Coefficient { get; set; }
    public double SkillFactor { get; set; }
    public override double TotalSalaryCost()
    {
        return Coefficient * 1000 + SkillFactor;
    }
}

public class QAEngineerSalary : Salary
{
    public double NumberOfHours { get; set; }
    public override double TotalSalaryCost()
    {
        return NumberOfHours * 700;
    }
}

public class TotalSalaryCost
{
    public double TotalSalary(Salary[] salaries)
    {
        double cost = 0;
        foreach (var salary in salaries)
        {
            cost += salary.TotalSalaryCost();
        }
        return cost;
    }
}
```

Here, we introduced one abstract class that is called *Salary*. This class contains only one method, which is abstract—*TotalSalaryCost*. The classes *SoftwareEngineerSalary* and *QAEngineerSalary* are still in the implementation. We have made the changes by making those two classes the subclasses of the *Salary* abstract class. So, the Salary class became the base class, and *SoftwareEngineerSalary* and *QAEngineerSalary* are now derived classes. In the derived classes, we have implemented the parent class abstract method. This way, employee type has its own total salary calculation implementation inside its own class. After these changes, *TotalSalaryCost* class is simplified. There is just one *foreach* statement where we have only one line of code. In each iteration, we just call the *TotalSalaryCost()* method over the current object in the loop. The objects in a loop are all of the Salary class type. The calculation of the salaries will jump into the correct implementation based on the object that is currently in the iteration cycle. All of this will be added and saved inside the **cost** variable. The result will then be returned through the variable *cost*, where the total amount is stored. Now, the open-closed principle is fulfilled. Each time we get a request to add a new employee and his salary calculation inside the program, we would just create a class for it and make it a subclass of a *Salary* class. We will then implement the abstract method, and that would be all.

The *TotalSalaryCost* class, where the iteration and summing of all salaries are happening, will stay untouched, and this is the goal of the entire process.

All of this can also be achieved with the use of an interface. The modified solution using an interface instead of the abstract class is given below:

```csharp
namespace OpenClosedPrinciple
{
    public interface ISalary
    {
        double TotalSalaryCost();
    }
    public class SoftwareEngineerSalary : ISalary
    {
        public double Coefficient { get; set; }
        public double SkillFactor { get; set; }
        public double TotalSalaryCost()
        {
            return Coefficient * 1000 + SkillFactor;
        }
    }

    public class QAEngineerSalary : ISalary
    {
        public double NumberOfHours { get; set; }
        public double TotalSalaryCost()
        {
            return NumberOfHours * 700;
        }
    }

    public class TotalSalaryCost
    {
        public double TotalSalary(ISalary[] salaries)
        {
            double cost = 0;
            foreach (var salary in salaries)
            {
                cost += salary.TotalSalaryCost();
            }
            return cost;
        }
    }
}
```

Instead of the abstract class, we now have an interface known as *ISalary*. Inside this interface, there is one method—the same method which was inside the abstract class in the previous example. The derived classes of the prior example are now implementing the *ISalary* interface, which means that they have their own implementation of the *TotalSalaryCost()* method exposed in the interface. In the *TotalSalaryCost* class, everything stayed the same; the only thing that is changed is the type of salaries variable, which is passed as a parameter to the *TotalSalary()* method. Now, instead of the abstract class as a type, we now have an *ISalary* interface that acts as a type for the classes that are implementing it. The result is completely the same, and the open-closed principle is fulfilled once again. Awesome, isn't it?

7.3 - Liskov

The LSP, or the Liskov Substitution Principle, says that all of the derived classes must be completely substitutable for their parent class. What this means is that if there is a class A that inherits from B, then the A class can be completely substitutable for class *B*. This principle states that all of the child classes should not affect the role of the superclass. So, derived classes should be entirely substitutable for their parent class. The Liskov Substitution Principle represents an extension of the previous principle—the open-closed principle. What this means is that the developer should ensure that the child classes are precisely extending the parent class without changing their behavior. Let's demonstrate this with an example:

```
using System;

namespace LiskovSubstitutionPrinciple
{
    class Program
    {
        static void Main(string[] args)
        {
            Truck truck = new Truck(3000, false);
            Console.WriteLine($"Truck bed capacity: {truck.BedCapacity}");
        }
    }

    class Truck:Vehicle
    {
        public int BedCapacity { get; }
        public Truck(int _BedCapacity, bool _IsAutomatic):base(_IsAutomatic)
        {
            BedCapacity = _BedCapacity;
        }
    }

    class Vehicle
    {
        public bool IsAutomatic { get; }
        public Vehicle(bool _IsAutomatic)
        {
            IsAutomatic = _IsAutomatic;
        }
    }
}
```

In this example, we can assume that there is no possible way that any of the members of the derived class can harm the behavior of the superclass. From the derived class, we can access both the *BedCapacity* property and the *IsAutomatic* property from its parent class without any potential abuse or problem. Every member is suitable for usage, and no exceptions are likely to happen. The problem could happen if we add one virtual

93

method to the base implementation and override that method in the derived class, but this will throw *NotImplementedException.* The code would look like this:

```csharp
using System;

namespace LiskovSubstitutionPrinciple
{
    class Program
    {
        static void Main(string[] args)
        {
            Truck truck = new Truck(3000, false);
            Console.WriteLine($"Truck bed capacity: {truck.Type()}");
        }
    }

    class Truck:Vehicle
    {
        public override string Type()
        {
            throw new NotImplementedException();
        }
        public int BedCapacity { get; }
        public Truck(int _BedCapacity, bool _IsAutomatic):base(_IsAutomatic)
        {
            BedCapacity = _BedCapacity;
        }
    }

    class Vehicle
    {
        public virtual string Type()
        {
            return "Vehicle";
        }
        public bool IsAutomatic { get; }
        public Vehicle(bool _IsAutomatic)
        {
            IsAutomatic = _IsAutomatic;
        }
    }
}
```

In this way, which is significantly wrong, we have the next logic: in the base class *Vehicle*, we added a virtual method with its core implementation—the *Type()* method. In the derived class, we have overridden that method, but with no implementation. We have thrown the *NotImplementedException* exception in the body of this method. This is wrong in many ways, and one of them is breaking the Liskov Substitution Principle. This is because, if the *Type()* method is called over the *Truck* object, it will throw an exception. So, it is not substitutable for the parent class Vehicle. It impairs the superclass functionality that is implemented, unlike the derived class functionality, which is obviously not implemented. As a result of this program, we will get an exception because we are trying to print the *Type()* to the console line over the *Truck* class object. Another example would look like this:

```csharp
using System;
using System.Collections.Generic;

namespace LiskovSubstitutionPrinciple
{
    class Program
    {
        static void Main(string[] args)
        {
            List<Worker> workers = new List<Worker>();
            workers.Add(new QAEngineer());
            workers.Add(new SoftwareDeveloper());
            foreach (Worker worker in workers)
            {
                worker.GetWorkerDetails(5);
            }
        }
    }

    public abstract class Worker
    {
        public virtual string GetTaskDetails(int employeeId)
        {
            return "Core Task";
        }
        public virtual string GetWorkerDetails(int employeeId)
        {
            return "Core Worker";
        }
    }
    public class QAEngineer : Worker
    {
        public override string GetTaskDetails(int employeeId)
        {
            return "QA Task";
        }

        public override string GetWorkerDetails(int employeeId)
        {
            return "QA Engineer Info";
        }
    }
    public class SoftwareDeveloper : Worker
    {
        public override string GetTaskDetails(int employeeId)
        {
            return "Developer Task";
        }

        public override string GetWorkerDetails(int employeeId)
        {
            throw new NotImplementedException();
        }
    }
}
```

In this example, we have a base class *Worker* that is marked as abstract. Inside this parent class, there are two virtual methods with their core implementations. The first one returns the details about the task on which the worker is currently working on. The second method returns information about the worker itself. Then there are two classes that represent the child classes of the *Worker* class. One of them is the *QAEngineer* class. Inside the *QAEngineer* class, there is the overridden implementation of the methods from the superclass. They both have normal definitions, so everything looks fine here. The other derived class is the *SoftwareDeveloper* class. In this class, there are also two overridden methods from the superclass. But here we can see one problem. The *GetWorkerDetails()* method does not have the implementation; it throws the Exception. For some reason, details may not be available for preview for software developers.

In the Main method, there is an iteration through the list of *Worker* type objects. In each iteration, the *GetWorkerDetails()* method is called over the current object. This looks good for the compiler, but what will actually happen? When the *SoftwareDeveloper* object gets into the iteration, and the *GetWorkerDetails()* method is called, the Exception is expected to be thrown. This is not what we want to happen, so we must make a derived class, completely substitutable for the superclass, which is not currently the case. The Liskov Substitution Principle is violated in this example. So, this solution would be next: introduce two interface components, one will contain the *GetWorkerDetails()* method—the *IWorker* interface, for example, and the second will contain the *GetTaskDetails()* method—the *ITask* interface. Suitable classes will implement none, one, or both of the given interfaces in order to accomplish the Liskov Substitution Principle. In this case, *QAEngineer* will be modified to implement both interfaces since it needs both methods to be implemented. The *SoftwareDeveloper* class will implement only the *ITask* interface because it only has the definition of the *GetTaskDetails()* method. This way, the Liskov Substitution Principle is fulfilled, and no violations would appear.

7.4 - Interface Segregation Principle

The Interface Segregation Principle states that entities should not be forced to implement interfaces they don't use. If possible, it is a lot better to create many simple and small interfaces that are based on a particular group of methods than to create one big interface with tons of methods that are not grouped at all. The interface should represent something that is tightly related to the entity that is using it. So, the interface must be defined based on the entity or entities that should implement it. The classes should not be obliged to depend on the interfaces that they don't use. Similar to that of the classes, the interfaces should have a particular responsibility. This could be referred to as the single responsibility principle. The class is not supposed to implement an interface if it is not sharing its complete design. While the interface is getting bigger and bigger, there is also a high chance of including the methods that not all implementers need to implement. To address this problem, the interface segregation principle detects the solution. An example of correct design in ISP aspect would be:

```csharp
using System;

namespace InterfaceSegregationPrinciple
{
    class Program
    {
        static void Main(string[] args)
        {
            Car car = new Car(1000);
            Truck truck = new Truck(3000);

            Console.WriteLine($"Car trunk capacity is: {car.TrunkCapacity}");
            Console.WriteLine($"Truck bed capacity is: {truck.BedCapacity}");
        }
    }

    public class Car : TrunkCapacity
    {
        public int TrunkCapacity { get; }

        public Car(int _TrunkCapacity)
        {
            TrunkCapacity = _TrunkCapacity;
        }
    }

    public class Truck : BedCapacity
    {
        public int BedCapacity { get; }

        public Truck(int _BedCapacity)
        {
            BedCapacity = _BedCapacity;
        }
    }

    public interface BedCapacity
    {
        int BedCapacity { get; }
    }

    public interface TrunkCapacity
    {
        int TrunkCapacity { get; }
    }
}
```

In this example, we have presented a correct way of design when considering the interface segregation principle. There are two interfaces, and they are the *BedCapacity* and *TrunkCapacity* interface. By convention, C# interfaces start with the letter "I" in their name; however, this example shows that it can be done without this prefix, but it is not recommended in production code. The *BedCapacity* has one read-only property of *int* data type—*BedCapacity*, and the *TrunkCapacity* interface also contains one read-only property of *int* data type—the *TrunkCapacity* property. The *Car* class implements the *TrunkCapacity* interface because a *Car* class only needs the implementation of the *TrunkCapacity* property. *Similarly*, the *Truck* class implements the *BedCapacity* interface since it only needs BedCapacity property to be implemented. This way, the interface segregation principle is totally fulfilled. We have two interfaces which are used to their maximum potential. Each of them is implemented only by the class that needs a particular implementation. We could create one interface and make both classes implement it, but that will not be correctly designed. In that single interface, there would be both properties that are currently split into two interfaces. This means that both classes must implement both properties, which is not needed at all. The *Car* class needs only the *TrunkCapacity* implementation, while the *Truck* class needs only the *BedCapacity* implementation, but that did not follow this principle. Another example can be as follows:

```
public interface IEmployee
{
    void CreateDevelopmentTask();
    void WorkOnDevelopmentTask();
}
public class Programmer : IEmployee
{
    public void CreateDevelopmentTask()
    {
        //Code to assign a task.
    }

    public void WorkOnDevelopmentTask()
    {
        //Code to implement perform assigned task.
    }
}
```

In this example, there is one interface *IEmployee*, and this interface contains two methods—*CreateDevelopmentTask()* and *WorkOnDevelopmentTask()*. Then we have a *Programmer* class that implements the above interface. Both methods from the interface have their implementation in the *Programmer* class. With this, everything now looks perfect. Later, if we get a request to insert a *Tester* class because testers can also be the employees in the company, we can create a Tester class and make it implement the *IEmployee* interface.

```
public class Tester : IEmployee
{
    public void CreateDevelopmentTask()
    {
        //Code to assign a task.
    }

    public void WorkOnDevelopmentTask()
    {
        throw new NotImplementedException();
    }
}
```

Looks good! The *CreateDevelopmentTask()* method has its implementation; the *Tester* is also able to create tasks for development. But what happens with the *WorkOnDevelopmentTask()* method? The *Tester* obviously is not supposed to work on the development tasks, so the *WorkOnDevelopmentTask()* method throws the exception called *NotImplementedException*. However, this does not follow the interface segregation principle. So, we must break this logic into two interface components and make their usage correct. The code will look like the example below:

```csharp
using System;

namespace InterfaceSegregationPrinciple
{
    public interface IProgrammer
    {
        void CreateDevelopmentTask();
        void WorkOnDevelopmentTask();
    }

    public interface ITester
    {
        void CreateDevelopmentTask();
    }
    public class Programmer : IProgrammer
    {
        public void CreateDevelopmentTask()
        {
            //Code to assign a task.
        }

        public void WorkOnDevelopmentTask()
        {
            //Code to implement perform assigned task.
        }
    }

    public class Tester : ITester
    {
        public void CreateDevelopmentTask()
        {
            //Code to assign a task.
        }
    }
}
```

Great! It looks better now. The interface segregation principle is now fulfilled. We have been able to divide the *IEmployee* interface into two more specific interface components. The first one is the *IProgrammer* interface, which contains both methods from the *IEmployee* interface. The second method is known as the *ITester* interface, and this interface contains only one method, and that is the *CreateDevelopmentTask()*. It does not have the *WorkOnDevelopmentTask()* method because the *Tester* class does not need it. The *Programmer* class will now implement the *IProgrammer* interface, and it will have full implementation of both methods from the interface. The *Tester* class will implement the *ITester* interface that contains only the *CreateDevelopmentTask()*

method. With these steps, we have been able to organize the interface usage better. There are no methods without implementations in any of the classes. Every new method that will be needed to add to either *Programmer* or *Tester* classes will find their way to the correct interface, and nothing will be unused. The interface segregation principle is completed in this example after a few modifications. The code is ready for new features, and it is easily possible to modify the behavior.

7.5 - Dependency Inversion Principle

"High-level modules should not depend upon the details, but on the abstraction." This sentence represents the dependency inversion principle. What this means is that there should not be tight coupling between software modules and components. Everything should be developed with the abstraction characteristic to avoid tight coupling. The high-level components are commonly implementing the business layer of a system, unlike the low-level components which are responsible for the more detailed procedures. The main thing here is that we must maintain high-level and low-level modules loosely coupled. In order to do so, there should not be an implementation that would make the two modules identify each other.

Tight coupling of the modules is when a high-level component knows a lot about other components with which it interacts. If there is tight coupling, there is also a big risk that the changes to one module or class will possibly break the logic in another module or class. There is a technique for the implementation of the dependency inversion principle in C#, and it is well-known as Inversion of Control (IoC). The inversion of control could be implemented by using abstract classes or interface components. This technique removes the dependencies between classes and modules. The low-level components should follow the commitment to a single interface, and the high-level components are supposed to use modules that are implementing that particular interface. Let's go over some examples:

```csharp
class Car:IVehicle
{
    public int TrunkCapacity { get; }
    public bool IsAutomatic { get; }
    public Car(int _TrunkCapacity, bool _IsAutomatic)
    {
        TrunkCapacity = _TrunkCapacity;
        IsAutomatic = _IsAutomatic;
    }
}

class Truck:IVehicle
{
    public int BedCapacity { get; }
    public bool IsAutomatic { get; }

    public Truck(int _BedCapacity, bool _IsAutomatic)
    {
        BedCapacity = _BedCapacity;
        IsAutomatic = _IsAutomatic;
    }
}

public interface IVehicle
{
    bool IsAutomatic { get; }
}



class Program
{
    static void Main(string[] args)
    {
        List<IVehicle> vehicles = new List<IVehicle>();

        Car car = new Car(1000,true);
        Truck truck = new Truck(3000,false);

        vehicles.Add(car);
        vehicles.Add(truck);

        Console.WriteLine($"Car is automatic: {vehicles[0].IsAutomatic}");
        Console.WriteLine($"Truck is automatic: {vehicles[1].IsAutomatic}");
        Console.WriteLine($"The cars trunk capacity is:
{((Car)vehicles[0]).TrunkCapacity}");
        Console.WriteLine($"The trucks bed capacity is:
{((Truck)vehicles[1]).BedCapacity}");
    }
}
```

In this example, there is an interface called *IVehicle*. Inside that interface, there is one property, which is the *IsAutomatic* read-only property. This interface is implemented by two classes. The first is known as the Car class. This class implements the *IsAutomatic* property from the interface and also contains one property of its own. The property that the *Car* class contains is the *TrunkCapacity*. Both properties are needed for instantiating the object of a Car class. The constructor takes two parameters, one for the *TrunkCapacity,* and the second for the *IsAutomatic* property.

The Truck class does something similar. It also implements the read-only property *IsAutomatic* from the interface, and it has a property of its own—the *BedCapacity*. Like in the previous class, here we also need both properties in order to create an instance of a *Truck* object. It is because the constructor takes two parameters, one for the *BedCapacity* assignment, and one for the *IsAutomatic* property assignment. In the *Main()* method of a program class, we have created an empty list of *IVehicle* elements. After that, we instantiated two objects, one object of a *Car* class type, and the other object of a *Truck* class type. Each of them implements the *IVehicle* interface so that they could be recognized as the *IVehicle* type. Due to this, we can then add those objects into the previously created list, and both of them are added to the list. After that, we print to the console line, the information about the vehicles from the list. We are printing the *IsAutomatic* information for both of the added objects, and also the *TrunkCapacity* for the *Car* object and *BedCapacity* for the *Truck* object. We are able to access this information by casting the object of the *IVehicle* type into the explicit object, and this is done for the *TrunkCapacity* writing and the *BedCapacity* writing.

For the *TrunkCapacity* information, we must cast an object to the *Car* object, while for the *BedCapacity*, we must cast an object to the *Truck* object. This program is following the dependency inversion principle because there are no tightly coupled components. For example, if we want to add a new class known as *Bicycle*, we would just create that class and force it to implement the *IVehicle* interface. The *Bicycle* class would have its own members, and it would implement the *IsAutomatic* property from the interface. This modification is not forcing us to change anything in the previously written code. This means that the components do not depend closely on each other. The *Bicycle* class object would be created and added to the list in the *Main()* method. After this, we can print the info about the *Bicycle* object. None of the statements which already exist need to be changed. The code in the *Main()* method of a *Program* class is loosely coupled with the components such as the *Car* and *Truck*.

Now, let's check out the second example:

```csharp
public interface IShape
{
    void Draw();
    void Stop();
}

public class Rectangle : IShape
{
    public void Draw()
    {
        Console.WriteLine("Drawing rectangle...");
    }

    public void Stop()
    {
        Console.WriteLine("Drawing rectangle stoppped.");
    }
}

public class Circle : IShape
{
    public void Draw()
    {
        Console.WriteLine("Drawing circle...");
    }

    public void Stop()
    {
        Console.WriteLine("Drawing circle stopped.");
    }
}


public class ShapeManager
{
    IShape _shape;

    public ShapeManager(IShape shape)
    {
        this._shape = shape;
    }

    public void DrawShape()
    {
        _shape.Draw();
    }

    public void StopDrawing()
    {
        _shape.Stop();
    }
}


class Program
{
    static void Main(string[] args)
    {
        IShape rectangle = new Rectangle();
        //IShape circle = new Circle();
        ShapeManager shapeManager = new ShapeManager(rectangle);
        shapeManager.DrawShape();
        shapeManager.StopDrawing();
    }
}
```

103

In this example, we have an interface called *IShape*, and inside this interface, there are two methods known as *Draw()* and *Stop()*. Below that interface, we have one class that implements the *IShape* interface—*Rectangle* class. This class has the implementation of the two methods from the interface.

In the *Draw()* method, the program will print that it is drawing the rectangle, while the *Stop()* method prints that the program stopped drawing the shape. This way the Rectangle class works in the same way the *Circle* class works. There is an implementation of both methods of the interface. The *Draw()* method prints that the program is drawing circles, and the *Stop()* method prints that the program stopped the drawing. So, these classes represent both the drawing shapes and stopping drawing shapes. It describes the control on when to start drawing and when to stop drawing. Below these classes, there is a *ShapeManager* class, which actually enacts the dependency inversion principle. In this class, we have one private field **_shape**, which is of *IShape* type. We assign the value to this private field in the constructor. This constructor takes one parameter, one *IShape* type object, and sets it to the private field value. This is called **dependency injection**. There are a few types of injection; they will all be covered in the Dependency Injection chapter later. For now, it is good to know that this is the constructor injection. In the runtime, when the object is created, we inject the value through the constructor. It is not known which kind of object will be set here until the injection.

In this case, two possible object types can be injected. The *_shape* field could become either a *Rectangle* object or the *Circle* object. Those two classes are currently implementing the *IShape* interface. After the constructor, there is a method called *DrawShape()*, whose function is to execute the *Draw()* method of the *_shape* variable. While looking at this method, we realize that it is not possible to know which implementation of the *Draw()* method will happen since we do not know the object that will be injected into the *_shape* variable. It can draw the *Rectangle* and the *Circle*.

Below *DrawShape()* method, there is also a *StopDrawing()* method, which calls the *Stop()* method of the *_shape* variable. It works on the same principle as the *DrawShape()* method. The implementation of the *StopDrawing()* depends on the injected object inside the variable *_shape*. Let's put all of these together. In the *Program* class, in the *Main()* method, we are creating an instance of the *Rectangle* class and putting it into the *IShape* variable type **rectangle**. Next, we instantiate an object of *ShapeManager* class, passing the rectangle variable to the creation. At this point, the injection happens, and the rectangle object value, which is a *Rectangle* class object, is assigned to the _shape field inside the *ShapeManager* class object. After this, we then call the *DrawShape()* method over the **shapeManager** object. This enacts the *Draw()* method of a *Rectangle* class because the object of the Rectangle class is injected into the private field of the *shapeManager*. So, it will print *"Drawing rectangle..."* to the console output. After the drawing, we call the *StopDrawing()* method over the *shapeManager* object. This results in calling the *Stop()* method from the *Rectangle* class as well because of the reason we explained above. So, it will print *"Drawing rectangle stopped."* to the console output. You may have noticed the commented line that is creating an instance of the *Circle* object. If you uncomment this line and put the circle object into the *ShapeManager* injection, you would get different values written to the standard output. These values will be from the *Circle* class method implementations. This example is showing the dependency inversion principle at its finest as there is no tight coupling of the modules.

For instance, we can easily add one more class known as *Triangle*, which would also implement the *IShape* interface. Then the *Triangle* object would also be possible to inject into the constructor of the *ShapeManager* class, and nothing in the *Main()* method should be changed. Loose coupling is achieved.

Chapter 8: Advanced Topics

In this advanced chapter, we will try to teach you how to handle more complex C# programming techniques. You will also learn more about what asynchronous programming is. Furthermore, you will get familiar with the parallel programming in C#. We will teach you other things like LINQ query syntax in C#, Dependency Injection design patterns, Mappers, and Object-relational mappers. By the time you're done with this chapter, you will be fully ready for some C# coding and testing your skills. Everything after this chapter depends on you. Enjoy the programming, and let's go!

8.1 - Asynchronous Programming

Asynchronous programming represents a way of handling events in the program. It happens when a single unit of work that represents some jobs or events runs separately from the main application thread. After execution, the event job will notify the thread that made the call about the success or failure execution. You are probably wondering when to use asynchronous programming and what kind of benefits it applies to your software. The biggest benefit of using the asynchronous programming technique is the improved responsiveness and performance of software. The operation, which is marked as asynchronous, is always running independently of the main process execution.

For example, in C#, a program starts executing the code from the *Main()* method, and after everything is finished, the program ends when the *Main()* method returns the value. All calls run sequentially, and every time, one operation waits until the previous operation finishes its job. The way asynchronous programming is done in C# is slightly different.

Here we are going to demonstrate the main principle. If you want to clarify the method to be asynchronous and force it to do the work asynchronously, you need to put the **async** keyword next to the access modifier. After that, you can call this function asynchronously. After you have prepared your function to work asynchronously, you would probably want to call it at some point. This is done by writing the keyword **await** in front of the method call. This means marking it to execute asynchronously.

Before getting to the examples, there are a few things you should know. In the runtime library in .Net that is used in a C# program, there are a few classes known as *System.Threading.Task* and *System.Threading.Task<T>*, and these classes let you create event tasks and make them run asynchronously. A task is something that represents the object in which some jobs should be done. The task is responsible for letting you know if the operation has some results. It is responsible for the completeness of the job. It also allows the creation of asynchronous logic that appears to be synchronous logic except for the keywords **async** and **await**. These keywords allow for easier maintenance of asynchronous logic compared to other methods of writing asynchronous logic like callback methods. To fully understand what tasks are, it is also essential to know what **threads** are. The C# .NET system library contains thread-associated classes in the *System.Threading* namespace. This namespace contains a set of components that are needed for asynchronous and parallel programming. A thread represents the small set of executable instructions and is represented by the class *System.Threading.Thread*. **Task** represents the return type of an asynchronous (async) method. Now, let us demonstrate this with an example:

```
class Program
{
    static void Main(string[] args)
    {
        Console.WriteLine("Hello World!");

        var response = SomeAsyncCode().Result;
        Console.WriteLine($"{response}");
    }

    private static async Task<string> SomeAsyncCode()
    {
        await Task.Delay(3000);
        return "All done!";
    }
}
```

In this small program, there is a simple demonstration of async programming. This example is not recommended for production code as it can cause deadlocks and is given only for illustration purposes. As always, there is a *Program* class with its *Main()* method inside. Besides the *Main()* method, there is one async method; an async task execution. This task returns a string in its result property. Inside the body of the *SomeAsyncCode()* method, there is an awaited call for the *Task.Delay()* method. This method waits the amount of time that is passed in the parameter before it returns the control to the calling thread. The amount of time is considered in milliseconds. This task will wait 3000 milliseconds, or 3 seconds before it returns the result string *"All done!"* In the *Main()* method, in the beginning, there is a simple output to the console saying *"Hello World!"* After that, there is a call to the task defined below and the assignment of its result to the variable response. In the end, there is a print to the console output of the result returned from the asynchronous task. What will actually happen here? You will see the *"Hello World!"* output to the console, and then there will be a delay of three seconds before the code continues the execution. After three seconds, the new output will be visible in the console. Let's run the program and show you the results:

Here is the *"Hello World!"* message. Wait three seconds: one, two, three. Boom! The final output is shown below:

After three seconds, we obtain the result of the async task—the "All done!" message, and the program came to an end. Let's demonstrate one more example to improve understanding:

```
class Program
{
    static void Main(string[] args)
    {
        AsyncMethod();
        NonAsyncMethod();
    }

    public static async Task AsyncMethod()
    {
        await Task.Run(() =>
        {
            for (int i = 0; i < 1000; i++)
            {
                Console.WriteLine("Async print");
            }
        });
    }

    public static void NonAsyncMethod()
    {
        for (int i = 0; i < 2500; i++)
        {
            Console.WriteLine("Non async print");
        }
    }
}
```

In this example, there are two methods. The first method is an async task method, which sets one task for asynchronous execution. Inside this async execution, there are one thousand iterations of printing the message *"Async print"* to the standard output. In the non-async method, there are two thousand and five hundred iterations of printing the *"Non async print"* message to the standard output. The *Main()* method contains the call to each of these methods, respectively. The first call is for the async method execution, and the second is for the normal execution. You can notice that there is no **await** keyword in front of the *AsyncMethod()* call in the *Main()* method. This means that this method will run asynchronously, but the execution of the statements below the async call will not wait until *AsyncMethod()* finishes its job. This will result in two jobs working in parallel. The first is the Main method thread, which will continue to the *NonAsyncMethod()* execution after running the async task for the *AsyncMethod()*. It will result in parallel printing of the different messages. There will be no order, as both threads will work on its own for each statement in parallel. It will provide an output as shown below:

109

It resulted in total print disorder. Those two threads were "competing" based on who will execute the job faster. But, if we modify the program a little bit, we can make it wait for the async method to finish. Below is the modified code:

```
static void Main(string[] args)
{
    ExecuteJob();
}

public static async void ExecuteJob()
{
    Task<int> task = AsyncMethod();
    NonAsyncMethod();
    int iterations = await task;
    Console.WriteLine(iterations);
}

public static async Task<int> AsyncMethod()
{
    int count = 0;
    await Task.Run(() =>
    {
        for (int i = 0; i < 1000; i++)
        {
            Console.WriteLine("Async print");
            count += 1;
        }
    });

    return count;
}

public static void NonAsyncMethod()
{
    for (int i = 0; i < 2500; i++)
    {
        Console.WriteLine("Non async print");
    }
}
```

110

Since the *Main()* method could not be marked as async, we created one async method *ExecuteJob()* and added the two methods from the previous example. First, we created a *Task<int>* reference from the *AsyncMethod()* and put it inside the **task** variable. The *NonAsyncMethod()* and *AsyncMethod()* were then executed. *AsyncMethod()* waits, and its result is printed after the execution is finished. The output is seen below:

8.2 - Parallel Programming

The parallel programming principle is the model in which the execution of the processes is divided into smaller pieces, which are to be done at the same time. This is also called concurrent programming.

It is realized by multiple processors (or cores of the processors) in order to accomplish better performance in the code execution. By splitting the operations to work concurrently, the time of task completion is reduced, which is obviously improving the performance, and the user's experience while working in a certain application. With the processor evolving, as a hardware device, the concurrent programming has taken its significant place in the programming.

The thing you must know is the concept of a thread. A thread represents the certain process execution for which a system is allocating the processor time. In concurrent programming, one process can have multiple threads that execute some action in Parallel if there are multiple CPUs or CPU cores in the hardware. The better the hardware, and the CPU components, the greater the possibility to execute some code in Parallel and to have results faster than with the usual technique.

111

It is important to define a few terms in C# that are linked with parallel programming. The **ConcurrentBag** represents a collection class that is supporting the data to be stored in some unordered manner. This class supports duplicates, and it is a thread-safe class that allows multiple threads to take advantage of it.

The **Parallel** class is the C# built-in class that provides support for loops working in parallel execution. Every looping statement we have used until now has executed the code in a sequential way. The Parallel class makes the loops execute their iterations in Parallel. There are also key methods, such as **Parallel.Invoke()**, **Parallel.For()**, and **Parallel.ForEach()**. Now we will show an example to further explain the concept of parallel programming:

```csharp
class Program
{
    static void Main(string[] args)
    {
        ConcurrentBag<int> parallelIntegers = new ConcurrentBag<int>();
        List<int> listIntegers = new List<int>();

        int numberOfIntegers = 5;
        while (numberOfIntegers-- > 0)
        {
            parallelIntegers.Add(numberOfIntegers);
            listIntegers.Add(numberOfIntegers);
        }


        Parallel.Invoke(
            () =>
            {
                listIntegers.ForEach(async integer =>
                {
                    System.Threading.Thread.Sleep(1000);
                });

                Console.WriteLine("Linear is done");
            },
            () =>
            {
                Parallel.ForEach(parallelIntegers, async integer =>
                {
                    System.Threading.Thread.Sleep(1000);
                });

                Console.WriteLine("Parallel is done");
            }

        );

    }
}
```

This program consists of one class *Program* and its *Main()* method. At the beginning of the program, we initialize one *ConcurrentBag* collection of integers. Below the *ConcurrentBag* collection, there is a simple list of *int* values object initialization. The *ConcurrentBag* object is called **parallelIntegers**, and the *List<int>* object is called **listIntegers**. After this, we created an *int* variable and assigned the value five to it.

112

This variable is used for populating the elements of both *parallelIntegers* and *listIntegers* variables. This is done through the *while* loop, which iterates five times because, in its condition, there is a decrementing of the **numberOfIntegers** variable in each iteration. The *numberOfIntegers* decrements each time the execution gets into the condition of a *while* loop. The value of the previously decremented variable is added to both the *parallelIntegers* and *listIntegers* collections. This means that both collections will have the next elements—*4, 3, 2, 1,* and *0*. After the collections are populated, we are then ready to execute some parallel code. The *Parallel.Invoke()* method is then called. This method takes an array of *Action* objects as a parameter. Each *Action* type represents a delegate, which is encapsulating a method, and it does not take any parameter. It is important to understand the delegates first. A delegate represents a pointer to a method, and it is a reference data type, and this reference is a reference to some method. Each *Action* delegate type can be used to pass a method as a parameter and all that is being done without declaring a custom delegate itself. In this example, the lambda expression is used to create Action objects. What are lambda expressions? This term in C# represents an anonymous function that contains an expression or sequence of statements or operators. The lambda expressions are using the lambda operator =>. This operator means something like: "The left side goes to something on the right side." The left side represents the input parameters of the lambda expression, and the right side contains the code block that works with the parameters passed on the right side. Lambda expressions are used to replace delegates when needed.

Now, let's return to the example. Here, in the *Parallel.Invoke()* method, we have two lambda expressions that are used as *Action objects*. On the left side, there is nothing— no parameters. This means that no parameters are passed to these lambda expressions. Both actions are supposed to execute in parallel. What are the *Action*s doing? In the first *Action* code block, there is a loop over each element of the **listIntegers** collection. In every iteration, the thread execution sleeps for 1000 milliseconds. This means that every iteration will wait for just one second before jumping to the next iteration. After the execution of the five iterations in this *listIntegers*, the program will print out to the console line the message, *"Linear is done"*. This means that the non-concurrent execution of the loop has finished its work. That will happen after about five seconds after the *Action* is invoked.

The second *Action* is a little bit different. Here we also have one lambda expression that represents the *Action*. This lambda expression also does not have any parameters passed to its code block. In the second *Action*, there is an iteration through the *ConcurrentBag* collection—*parallelIntegers*. For each element of this collection, the program sleeps for 1000 milliseconds (one second). The main difference is that this loop is made concurrently. Every iteration starts at about the same time and will be executed

113

separately. The code block of this loop also sleeps in the program for one second. But, if five iterations start at about the same time, and the job of every iteration is to wait for one second, what will actually happen? The thing is that those five separate threads will all start at the same time, and each of them will wait for one second. This will produce the one-second wait for all of the five iterations. So, this loop will be executed in about one second. We can conclude that this second *Action* will be finished in one-second time, which is obviously not the case with the first *Action*. The first *Action* will last about five seconds because every iteration is executed sequentially and non-concurrently. The final output of this program will be the *"Parallel is done"* message—after the approximate one-second wait, and then the *"Linear is done"* message after the approximate five second wait. Let's run the program and prove these statements.

The second *Action* finished the execution after about one second. Let's wait for the first *Action* to finish its execution. One, two, three, four, five... Boom!

The second message is also printed to the console output, and the program finished the execution. With this, we have demonstrated the parallel programming concept. Pretty cool, right?

8.3 - LINQ

Language integrated query, better known as LINQ, represents query syntax in C#, and it is used for retrieval and filtering of the different sources of objects. LINQ produces a single querying interface for various kinds of objects and variables. This query syntax is integrated into C#, as well as in Visual Basic. To improve understanding, we will provide an example to further explain it. Therefore, you have SQL as a Structured Query Language. SQL is used to get and save data into a database. It is a language designed to work closely with a database.

In the same way as SQL, LINQ is used to get and filter different data sources like collections, data sets, etc. There are many ways you can use LINQ; it is used to query object collections, ADO .Net data sets, XML Documents, Entity Framework Core data sets, SQL database direct, and other data sources by implementing the *IQuerable* interface. LINQ is like a bridge between some data and variables in the program. Every LINQ query returns objects as a result. It is good because it enables the use of an object-oriented approach on the data set. When using LINQ, you do not need to worry about converting the setups of data into objects. LINQ provides a way to query data wherever that data came from. It supports compile-time syntax checking, so that if you make a mistake while coding LINQ, the compiler will inform you immediately. LINQ allows you to query every collection such as *List and Array classes*, etc. It also allows you to query interfaces like the *IEnumerable* interface.

115

We will review the examples now:

```csharp
class Program
{
    static void Main(string[] args)
    {
        List<Car> cars = new List<Car>()
        {
            new Car(100,true,false),
            new Car(200,false,true),
            new Car(300,true,true),
            new Car(400,false,false),
            new Car(500,false,true)
        };

        var carsThatAreAutomatic = cars.Where(s => s.IsAutomatic).ToList();

        carsThatAreAutomatic.ForEach(carThatIsAutomatic =>
        {
            Console.WriteLine($"The car with the trunk capacity of {carThatIsAutomatic.TrunkCapacity} is automatic");
        });
    }
    class Car
    {
        public int TrunkCapacity { get; }
        public bool IsAutomatic { get; }
        public bool IsTurboCharged { get; }

        public Car(int _trunkCapacity, bool _isAutomatic, bool _isTurboCharged)
        {
            TrunkCapacity = _trunkCapacity;
            IsAutomatic = _isAutomatic;
            IsTurboCharged = _isTurboCharged;
        }
    }
}
```

In this example, we have one class named *Car*. In the *Car* class, there are three properties, which are the *TrunkCapacity*, *IsAutomatic*, and *IsTurboCharged*. Each property represents the read-only property, and their initial state is set in the *Car* class constructor. The constructor takes three parameters and assigns their values to the properties mentioned above. In the *Main()* method, we are creating a list of *Car* objects. The list of *Car* objects is populated in the declaration part, creating five *Car* objects with different values for the *TrunkCapacity*, *IsAutomatic*, and *IsTurboCharged* properties. After this, we filter the list and take only cars that have automatic transmission. This will be done by using the LINQ query. We create an object named **carsThatAreAutomatic** and filter the **cars** list with LINQ. Then we perform the **Where()** LINQ extension method to get the objects that we need. How does it work? In the *Where()* method, we declare an iterative variable that will be used for filtering conditions.

The variable in this example is **s**. So, what the filter does next is that for every *s* object in the cars list, it will grant us the object whose *s.IsAutomatic* property is equal to true. This will, in turn, create a filtered *IEnumerable* list. In order to make this a list of explicit type objects, we will do the simple *ToList()* method over the filtered *IEnumerable* list. This will create an object of *List<Car>* type and put it into the **carsThatAreAutomatic** object. Now, we have the data that we need. In the end, we will iterate through the newly created collection of *Car* objects and print messages to the console output. For every object in the list, we will print *"The car with the trunk capacity of {certain* *capacity} is automatic"*. We know this because we filtered the *cars* and took only the ones who have automatic transmission. The output of this program looks like this:

As you can see, there are two cars with automatic transmission and their capacity is 100 and 300 respectively. You can check that in the creation of the *Car* list at the beginning, as only the first and the third car have the true value for the *IsAutomatic* property passed in the object instantiation.

Another example is shown below:

```
class Program
{
    static void Main(string[] args)
    {
        List<Person> people = new List<Person>()
        {
            new Person(1200,"Mark","Pent"),
            new Person(3400,"Peter","Parker"),
            new Person(2300,"Julian","Stones"),
            new Person(5000,"Mike","Deen"),
            new Person(3250,"Catrin","Burns")
        };

        var seniors = people.Where(s => s.Salary > 3000).ToList();
        var seniorSalaries = seniors.Select(x => x.Salary).ToList();
        var seniorSalariesSum = 0;
        seniorSalaries.ForEach(seniorSalary => seniorSalariesSum += seniorSalary);
        Console.WriteLine($"The sum of all senior salaries is { seniorSalariesSum }");
    }

    class Person
    {
        public int Salary { get; }
        public string FirstName { get; }
        public string LastName { get; }
        public Person(int Salary, string FirstName, string LastName)
        {
            this.Salary = Salary;
            this.FirstName = FirstName;
            this.LastName = LastName;
        }
    }
}
```

In this example, we have a class named *Person*. This class has three properties, which are *Salary*, *FirstName*, and *LastName*. Each Person object represents one employee with its basic information. The object's properties are assigned in the constructor. In the *Main()* method, there is a creation of a list with objects of the *Person* class type. We have added five Person objects, each with different salary amounts, first names, and last names. The manager wants to filter out everyone who has a salary greater than 3000, and these people will be marked as seniors. We will do this with the LINQ query. As in the previous example, we are filtering the people list with the *Where()* extension method. In this method, we are declaring that we want only the Person objects that have a Salary greater than 3000. After the retrieval is done, the *ToList()* method takes the filtered *IEnumerable* list into the seniors objects list. Now we have an object that is a list of Person class types, and it contains only the people who have a *Salary* greater than *3000*. This variable is named **seniors**. Now the manager requests that he wants the total sum of the senior salaries. We will then do that by creating a list of senior salaries and then summing all of the values into one variable and end up printing it to the standard output. The creation of the **seniorSalaries** list will be done with the execution of the *Select()* LINQ extension method. The *Select()* method is used when there is a need to get only certain property values from a collection of objects. In this case, we need the Salary property value from each of the objects inside the *seniors* list. The *Select()* method does the following: for each **x** object from the *seniors* list, take **x.Salary** value. This creates a list of *IEnumerable* values. After the *ToList()* method execution, we succeed in creating a *List<int>* object that contains elements that are senior salaries. Then we create a variable in which we will store the summation of all of the senior salaries—**seniorSalariesSum** variable. After this is done, we have one more statement that will finish the work. The *ForEach()* method is done over the *seniorSalaries* list, which will gather and sum all salaries into one variable *seniorSalariesSum*. In the end, the program will print the result—*seniorSalariesSum* value to the standard output. The output of this program will look like this:

This logic and solution to the problem can be simplified, and the senior salary sum can be done in just one line of code. That line can look like this:

```
var seniorSalariesSum = 0;
people.Where(s => s.Salary > 300).Select(x => x.Salary).ToList().ForEach(salary =>
seniorSalariesSum += salary);

Console.WriteLine($"The sum of all senior salaries is { seniorSalariesSum }");
```

After the *Where()* method is executed, the *Select()* method would follow, after which the *List* will be created over which we could iterate with the *ForEach()* extension method and do the sum calculation. This will produce the exact same result. This big statement is just split into a few smaller ones in the starting solution for better understanding. Let us close this LINQ chapter with one more example:

119

```
class Program
{
    static void Main(string[] args)
    {
        List<Person> people = new List<Person>()
        {
            new Person(1200, new PersonalInformation("Mark","Pent", 123)),
            new Person(3400, new PersonalInformation("Peter","Parker", 155)),
            new Person(2300, new PersonalInformation("Julian","Stones", 133)),
            new Person(5000, new PersonalInformation("Mike","Deen", 143)),
            new Person(3250, new PersonalInformation("Catrin","Burns", 205))
        };

        var seniorsLT150 = people.Where(x => x.Salary > 3000)
                            .Select(x => x.PersonalInformation)
                            .Where(x => x.PersonalID < 150)
                            .Select(x => x.FirstName).ToList();

        seniorsLT150.ForEach(seniorFirstName =>
            Console.WriteLine($"Senior name is { seniorFirstName }")
        );
    }
}

class Person
{
    public int Salary { get; }
    public PersonalInformation PersonalInformation{ get; }
    public Person(int salary, PersonalInformation personalInformation)
    {
        Salary = salary;
        PersonalInformation = personalInformation;
    }
}

class PersonalInformation
{
    public string FirstName { get; }
    public string LastName { get; }
    public int PersonalID { get; }
    public PersonalInformation(string firstName, string lastName, int personalID)
    {
        FirstName = firstName;
        LastName = lastName;
        PersonalID = personalID;
    }
}
```

In this example, we have modified the *Person* class from the previous example. Now, the *Person* class contains the *Salary* property and *PersonalInformation* class type property, and both are assigned in the Person class constructor. The *PersonalInformation* class contains three read-only properties. These properties are *FirstName*, *LastName*, and *PersonalID*. *FirstName* and *LastName* are of a string data type, while the *PersonalID* is of an *int* data type. These three properties are assigned in the constructor when instantiating the object of *PersonalInformation* class. Now, let's jump into the *Main()* method of the *Program* class. Here, we are again going to create a list of *Person* objects, and it is the same as in the previous example. Though, this time it is going to be a bit different because of the *Class* modifications. We are creating five *Person* objects, each of them with *Salary*, and *PersonalInformation* objects assigned.

For every Person, we create a *PersonalInformation* object to instantiate the Person object correctly. Each of the *PersonalInformation* objects has the first name, last name, and personal ID passed to its instantiation. This way, we created a bit more complex object that contains another class object inside. Ok, we are ready to go! The manager asks us to find every first name of an employee who is treated as a senior and has a personal ID of less than 150. From the previous example, we have acknowledged that the senior is the *Person* with a *Salary* greater than three thousand (*3000*). We are doing something similar to the previous example, but this time, the Person class has changed. It does not have the same structure as in the previous example. So, we must analyze the class structure first and then create a solution. The first step is that we must filter the *Person* objects from the people list that have a *Salary* greater than *3000*. After that, we must take the *PersonalInformation* object from every *Person* object in order to find the first names of all the seniors. Then, when *PersonalInformation* objects are gathered, we must filter them and take only the ones with the *PersonalID* that are less than *150*. When that task is done, we can finally select the *FirstName* property of all the seniors, make a list out of it, iterate through the list, and print the *FirstName* values. All of this is done in the little complex LINQ query from which we create a **seniorsLT150** list variable. The first *Where()* method creates an *IEnumerable* list of seniors. Then, the *Select()* method takes *PersonalInformation* objects from seniors list and makes an *IEnumerable* list of the seniors *PersonalInformation* objects. The second *Where* method is working over the *PersonalInformation* objects from the previously created *IEnumerable* list, and there we will filter the *PersonalInformation* object that has a *PersonalID* property less than *150*. From there, we will do the *Select()* method, which gathers the *FirstName* property value for each of the seniors *PersonalInformation* objects that has *PersonalID* less than *150*. In the end, we then execute the *ToList()* method over the final *IEnumerable* that we created, and the final product is the list of strings that contain the first name of every senior with a personal *ID* less than *150*. When all of this is finally queried, we can run through the list and print those names to the console. The only senior who will meet these criteria is Mike Dean, and his first name will be printed to the standard output. The program console output is shown below:

8.4 - Generics

The principle of defining classes and methods with the placeholder represents a generic term in C#. The main concept of the generics is to allow every type in C# to act as a parameter to methods, classes, interfaces, etc. When talking about collections, there is one important limitation, and that is the absence of effective type checking. What this means is that any object can be put inside a collection. This is because all class types in C# programming language inherit from the base class Object. All of this can evolve to a significant performance impact because of the implicit and explicit typecasting, which is required to add or get the objects from a collection. Type-safety is the basic definition of the C# as a programming language, but this contradicts that claim. To address this problem, the .NET runtime and C# programming language provides generics to create classes, interfaces, methods, and structures programmatically. In the C# and the .NET runtime, there are an extensive set of interfaces and classes which are built in. They are located in the *System.Collections.Generic* namespace, and there you can find the implementation of the generic collections.

Probably one of the most powerful features in C# is the usage of generics. With it, you can define the type-safe data structures. With generics usage, it is possible to create classes and methods that lack the data type until the class or method is declared and instantiated by the client service code implementation. Generics are powerful because they decrease the need for boxing, unboxing, type-casting the objects, etc. The only thing that is specified in the generic class creation is parameter types. The boxing and unboxing terms are probably something you should also learn about when dealing with C#. Boxing represents the execution of the conversion of the value type to the reference type, or to the interface that is implemented by this value type.

For example:
  int numb = 7;
  object objNumb = numb;

In this example, the *int* variable *numb* is boxed and assigned to the object variable **objNumb**.

Unboxing is the process of extracting the value type from the object itself.

For example:

  objnumb = 7;
  numb = (int)objNumb;

In this example, the object **objNumb** is then unboxed and assigned to a string variable word.

The example of the generic class usage is given below:

```csharp
public class GenericClass<T>
{
    private T information;

    public T Result
    {
        get
        {
            return this.information;
        }
        set
        {
            this.information = value;
        }
    }
}

class Program
{
    static void Main(string[] args)
    {
        GenericClass<int> number = new GenericClass<int>();
        number.Result = 10;

        GenericClass<bool> condition = new GenericClass<bool>();
        condition.Result = true;

        GenericClass<string> text = new GenericClass<string>();
        text.Result = "Test";

        Console.WriteLine(number.Result);
        Console.WriteLine(condition.Result);
        Console.WriteLine(text.Result);
    }
}
```

In this example, you can see the generic class named *GenericClass* with its *T* type parameter. *T* represents a type that will be replaced with the concrete object type when this class will be instantiated. In this class, we have created one simple generic usage over the encapsulation with the public property and one private field, which is controlled in full control of the property. The private field is of a *T* type, which means that it could be whatever type passed, and its name is **information**. Then, there is a public property named **Result**, and it is also of a *T* type, the generic type. In this generic type property, there are the get and the set accessors which are responsible for retrieving the *information* value and setting the value to the *information* field, respectively. The usage is demonstrated in the *Main()* method of a *Program* class. First, we use the *GenericClass* class to instantiate an *int* class type. This is done by replacing the *T* type with a real object type when creating the object of a generic class. As you can see, here, the *int* type is provided as a parameter when the number variable is instantiated. After the **number** variable is instantiated, we then access the *Result* property of that object in order to set the value 10 to the private field. When the number 10 landed inside, this *set* accessor concludes that the type of property is an integer, and that type will also be transferred to the field. Next, there is an instantiation of the **condition** object that is also created with the usage of *GenericClass*, with the *bool* type as the parameter specified. So, this object will be a *GenericClass* object with a *bool* parameter type. It means that it expects a *bool* type to be assigned to the property *Result*, which is done in the next line. The *true* value is set to the *Result* property, which leads the *true* value set into the information field. Lastly, we created the *GenericClass* object of a *string* type, because the string is passed as a parameter when the instantiation happens. We then assigned the *"Test"* string value to the *Result* property. When the objects are instantiated, and the *Result* property is set inside each of them, we are ready for the printing. The program will print the value of a *Result* property from each of the objects. When this program runs, the console output will look like this:

```
Microsoft Visual Studio Debug Console                          —    □    ×
10
True
Test

C:\Users\LENOVO\Desktop\EBOOK C#\EBOOK C#\Outline Problem Examples\Collections\bin\Debug\netcoreapp3.1\Collections.exe (
process 20544) exited with code 0.
To automatically close the console when debugging stops, enable Tools->Options->Debugging->Automatically close the conso
le when debugging stops.
Press any key to close this window . . .
```

Besides generic classes, you can also declare generic methods. Generic methods are those that take the generic types in an argument and execute some logic with them inside the method. There is a possibility to pass a familiar type with a generic type as method arguments. Let's review a generic method example:

```csharp
public class TestGenericMethod
{
    public void MiddleValue<T>(string text, T value, string text2)
    {
        Console.WriteLine($"The generic value between the {text} and {text2} is
{value}");
    }
}

class Program
{
    static void Main(string[] args)
    {
        TestGenericMethod p = new TestGenericMethod();
        p.MiddleValue("FIRST PARAMETER", 122.53, "SECOND PARAMETER");
        p.MiddleValue("FIRST PARAMETER", true, "SECOND PARAMETER");
        p.MiddleValue("FIRST PARAMETER", "GENERIC", "SECOND PARAMETER");
    }
}
```

In this example, you can see one class named *TestGenericMethod*. In this class, there is only one member. That member is a method that is defined as generic. The *MiddleValue<T>()* is declared as generic because it has one generic argument named value. Besides this generic argument, the method takes two more parameters, which are passed as a familiar type. The generic parameter is passed as a middle parameter, so it is the second of three passed parameters. The *MiddleValue<T>()* method has one task, and this is to print the generic parameter value to the console by stating that this parameter is between the first and the last parameter passed. In the *Main()* method of a *Program* class, there is a demonstration of this generic method usage. The first thing that is done is the instantiation of the *TestGenericMethod* object in order to call its generic method. This object is stored in the variable *p*. Then, we call the *MiddleValue<T>()* method three times over the object *p* each time we are passing the different type of the parameter in the generic type parameter.

The first time, we passed the *122.53* value, which is a *double* data type. This generic method will recognize this value as a *double* data type, and it will execute the console print of that argument as a *double*. In the second call to the *MiddleValue<T>()* method, there is a *true* value passed as a generic parameter. The method will recognize this value as a *bool* data type and will act as the middle parameter of the *bool* data type when doing a console print. Lastly, there is a call to the *MiddleValue<T>()* method with a *"GENERIC"* string value as a second parameter. This will be treated as the string data type passed to the method, and the program will print the message using all three variables passed as a string data type variable. The output of this program will look like this:

Similarly, as you can declare generic classes and methods, you can also declare generic delegates. Let us review an example that shows generic delegate usage:

```
delegate T DelegateCalcTest<T>(T parameter);
public static class DelegateGenericDemonstration
{
    static int num = 1;

    public static int NumValue()
    {
        return num;
    }
    public static int CalculateExpression(int p)
    {
        num += 10*p;
        return num;
    }
    public static int AssignNum(int q)
    {
        num = q;
        return num;
    }
}

public class Program
{
    static void Main(string[] args)
    {
        DelegateCalcTest<int> assignDelegate =
            new DelegateCalcTest<int>(DelegateGenericDemonstration.AssignNum);
        DelegateCalcTest<int> calcDelegate =
            new
DelegateCalcTest<int>(DelegateGenericDemonstration.CalculateExpression);

        assignDelegate(25);
        Console.WriteLine("Value of Num: {0}",
            DelegateGenericDemonstration.NumValue());

        calcDelegate(5);
        Console.WriteLine("Result of the calculation: {0}",
            DelegateGenericDemonstration.NumValue());
    }
}
```

In this example, we have exposed generic delegate usage. In the beginning, there is a delegate definition, it is of a *T* type, with a *T* type parameter, so it represents a generic delegate. After the delegate declaration, we created a static class named *DelegateGenericDemonstration*. Inside this class, there is one field that is also static, which means that its value state will always be remembered when manipulated over this class. This field's name is *num*, and it is set to the value *1* in the declaration. The first method inside this class is the static method *NumValue()*, which returns the current value of the static field *num*. Then, there is an implementation of the *CalculateExpression()* method. This method takes one argument and performs the following calculation: the passed value is multiplied by ten, and then we add the *num* variable value to the multiplication. After the addition is done, we store this newly calculated value inside the *num* field again and return it to the caller. The last method is *AssignNum()*, which also takes one argument. The value passed to the method is then assigned to the num field variable and returned to the caller. Now, we will put these methods to use with the delegate *DelegateCalcTest<T>*.

As we have mentioned earlier, delegates represent the pointers to the methods. So, we will create delegates that will be defined as a pointer to the methods from the *DelegateGenericDemonstration* class. Firstly, we will instantiate the *assignDelegate*, which will be of an *int* data type. This delegate is defined to be a pointer to the *AssignNum()* method from the *DelegateGenericDemonstration* static class. The second delegate that is created is the *calcDelegate*, which is also of an *int* data type. The *calcDelegate* will represent a pointer to the *CalculateExpression()* method. Now that we defined the delegates, we can put them to use and execute methods. We then execute the *assignDelegate* call with the parameter value of *25* passed. At this moment, delegate activates the execution of the *AssignNum()* method because it points to it. The delegate passes the parameter *25* to the *AssignNum()* method, and what happens is that the value *25* is then assigned to the static field *num* from the *DelegateGenericDemonstration* class.

After the delegate call, we print the current value of the *num* variable with a call to the *NumValue()* method from the static class. This will return the previously assigned value, which will be *25*. So, the console output will be *"Value of Num: 25"*. Next, we call the *calcDelegate* execution with the parameter value five passed to its execution. This will jump to the execution of the *CalculateExpression()* method from the static class because the delegate points to it. It passes the parameter value *5* to the method, which results in the following calculation. The parameter value is multiplied by ten, and the current value in the *num* variable is added to it. This calculated value is then stored in the *num* static variable. So, 10*5=50 plus the current value in the *num* variable, which is equal to *25* because of the previous delegate execution. The final addition, which is stored to the *num* variable, is 50+25=75. Finally, we print the result of the calculation onto the console output by calling the *GetNum()* method from the static class. It will print the message, *"Result of the calculation: 75"* to the console. After the program is run, we will get this result:

```
Microsoft Visual Studio Debug Console                                — □ ×
Value of Num: 25
Result of the calculation: 75

C:\Users\LENOVO\Desktop\EBOOK C#\EBOOK C#\Outline Problem Examples\Collections\bin\Debug\netcoreapp3.1\Collections.exe (
process 13128) exited with code 0.
To automatically close the console when debugging stops, enable Tools->Options->Debugging->Automatically close the conso
le when debugging stops.
Press any key to close this window . . .
```

8.5 - Dependency Injection

Dependency Injection (DI) represents a design pattern which is probably one of the most frequently used design patterns in C# programming. The dependency injection design pattern is used for the implementation of the Inversion of Control (IoC). What dependency injection does is that it allows the creation of the dependent entities outside of a class. It makes us provide those objects to the concrete component in different ways. The binding and creation of the objects that are marked as dependent are moved outside of the class that depend on those objects. In order to achieve this, dependency injection implementation is needed. DI allows us to implement loose coupling between software modules. In fact, it helps us prevent the tight coupling between software modules, which can make development more complex even for small changes and features.

When there is correct implementation of the dependency injection in the application or software, then we can easily implement future changes and requests from clients. Our application will be more maintainable and flexible for changes. Before we continue, we should first recall what tight coupling and loose coupling are. When a lot of classes or components depend on each other, that means that they are tightly coupled. In other words, if two software modules depend on each other, and we need to change the dependent object, then there will also be a need to change the module where the dependent object is used. And of course, we do not want that to happen. In big applications that are on the enterprise level, this kind of mistake is unacceptable because it can lead to major modifications throughout the software modules. In small applications, this problem would probably not be too hard to solve, but on the enterprise level, the complexity can be enormous.

129

Unlike tight coupling, loose coupling is when software modules or components do not depend on each other. In other words, if there is a change inside one module, we are not forced to change the logic inside the other module. That is what every software architect tries to achieve when designing the application. When you have loosely coupled software, it is easy to make changes and manage the new features. In the dependency injection design pattern, there are three types of classes included in the implementation.

The first class type used is the *Client* class. The client class represents a dependent class, and it depends on the *Service* class. The service class is the second type of class needed inside dependency injection implementation. The *Service* class represents a dependency, and it provides the dependency service to the *Client* class. The last class needed in DI is the Injection class. The job of the Injection class is to inject the *Service* class object into the *Client* class. There are three possible ways of injection. The first dependency injection type is through the class constructor, and it is called the **Constructor Injection**. The main thing about the Constructor Injection is that it does not contain any default states. Only the specified values are required to instantiate the object. The Constructor Injection uses the parameters from the constructor to inject the dependency into some field or property in a class, and it is possible to use the injected object anywhere within the class. The Constructor Injection is the most popular, and the one you'll probably see most of the time. There are many advantages to using the Constructor Injection, and the most significant one is for unit-testing support. It is the best solution when doing unit and integration testing of software modules.

The second type of dependency injection is **Property Injection**. This type of injection is also called Setter Injection because it is done through *set* accessor of the property. It helps us create injected objects as late as possible. There is only one minor problem in this type of injection, which is the difficulty of identifying the dependencies that are needed. The null checker is required before using the Property Injection if object that is being injected into is not known to exist. A null checker is a piece of code that checks for null. The null checker is not needed if the object is known to exist at all times, as this case. The advantage is that it does not depend on adding or changing the constructors in the class.

The last type of injection is **Method Injection**. It is an injection that is not used very frequently. It is only needed for some edge cases. How does it work? The injection happens in the class method itself. The dependency is to be utilized by that particular method. This is useful in a case when a whole class requires only one method and not the whole dependency.

For each of these injection types, we will provide an example. Let us start with an example showing the most popular and the most used type—the Constructor Injection:

```csharp
public interface IService
{
    void PrintMessage();
}
public class ConfirmationMessageService : IService
{
    public void PrintMessage()
    {
        Console.WriteLine("Confirm injection");
    }
}
public class DeclineMessageService : IService
{
    public void PrintMessage()
    {
        Console.WriteLine("Decline injection");
    }
}
public class MessageManager
{
    private IService _service;
    public MessageManager(IService service)
    {
        this._service = service;
    }
    public void Print()
    {
        this._service.PrintMessage();
    }
}

class Program
{
    static void Main(string[] args)
    {
        ConfirmationMessageService msgService = new ConfirmationMessageService();
        MessageManager msgManager = new MessageManager(msgService);
        msgManager.Print();

        DeclineMessageService msgService2 = new DeclineMessageService();
        msgManager = new MessageManager(msgService2);
        msgManager.Print();
    }

}
```

In this example, we will demonstrate the Constructor Injection type of the Dependency Injection design pattern. We have one interface called *IService*. This interface component contains one method signature—*PrintMessage()*. This method will be implemented inside Service classes. The first Service class is the *ConfirmationMessageService*, which is implementing the *IService* interface and contains its implementation of the interface component method *PrintMessage()*. In the state of the *ConfirmationMessageService* class, this method will print out to the standard output message *"Confirm injection"*. The next Service class is the *DeclineMessageService* class,

131

which also implements the *IService* interface. Inside this class, there is a different implementation of the *PrintMessage()* method from the interface. In this implementation, we have the message, *"Decline injection"* printed onto the console output. The next thing to do is to create a *Client* class. The *Client* class, in this example, is the *MessageManager* class. This class contains one private field _service, which represents the *IService* type object. This object is supposed to be injected over the constructor when creating an object of the *MessageManager* class. The constructor of this class takes one parameter, and that parameter is the *IService* type object, which will be injected into the private field _service. What we also have in this class is the *Print()* method. The *Print()* method calls the *PrintMessage()* method execution over the injected *IService* object.

So, there are two possible implementations where this call could jump to. It could jump to the *ConfirmationMessageService* class implementation of the *PrintMessage()* or to the *DeclineMessageService* class implementation of the *PrintMessage()* method. The Constructor Injection is demonstrated in the *Main()* method of the Program class. Here, we created an object of the *ConfirmationMessageService* class. This object is then passed to the constructor when creating the *MessageManager* object. At that particular moment, the dependency injection is happening. The *msgManager* object has the *msgService* object injected into the _service field of its own class. Now, when calling the *Print()* method over the *msgManager* variable, the *PrintMessage()* method of a *ConfirmationMessageService* class will be executed. This will result in a *"Confirm injection"* message printed to the standard output.

After this, we create an object of the *DeclineMessageService* class to inject that object into the *MessageManager* object and demonstrate the dependency injection with the different class type. The *msgManager* variable reference is changed to the newly instantiated object, which is now with the *DeclineMessageService* object injection. This time the _service field will be injected with the different class type object (*DeclineMessageService* object). So, now, when the *Print()* method is called over the *msgManager* variable, the *PrintMessage()* implementation of the *DeclineMessageService* class will be executed. This will result in the printing of the *"Decline injection"* message to the standard output. Now, let's run the program and check the results.

The results are as expected. The constructor injection is achieved with two different class type objects.

Now, let us demonstrate the Property Injection (or Setter Injection) type of Dependency Injection.

```
public interface IService
{
    void PrintMessage();
}
public class ConfirmationMessageService : IService
{
    public void PrintMessage()
    {
        Console.WriteLine("Confirm injection");
    }
}
public class DeclineMessageService : IService
{
    public void PrintMessage()
    {
        Console.WriteLine("Decline injection");
    }
}
public class MessageManager
{
    private IService _service;
    public IService Service
    {
        set { this._service = value; }
    }
    public void Print()
    {
        this._service.PrintMessage();
    }
}

class Program
{
    static void Main(string[] args)
    {
        ConfirmationMessageService msgService = new ConfirmationMessageService();
        MessageManager msgManager = new MessageManager();
        msgManager.Service = msgService;
        msgManager.Print();

        DeclineMessageService msgService2 = new DeclineMessageService();
        msgManager.Service = msgService2;
        msgManager.Print();
    }

}
```

In this example, we have modified the previous solution in order to achieve the Property Injection type of Dependency Injection. The interface component stayed the same, as well as the *Service* classes. Their functionality and usage should stay the same as in the previous example. Objects of those classes should just be injected into the property of a *Client* class this time, instead of the injection into the constructor. In the Client class, there is still a private field _service_ that is of the *IService* object type. Next, there is no more custom constructor where we injected the value in the previous example of a Constructor Injection type. Instead of the constructor, we have one public property, which is in control of the private field _service_. This property has a setter accessor, and there the property injection will happen. The value passed to the property assignment will be set as a private field value of the _service_ variable. After this is done, the *Print()* method could be called over the previously instantiated *MessageManager* object. Notice that, if you do not inject the value to the public property of a *MessageManager* object, you won't be able to call the *Print()* method. In fact, you will be able to call that method, but you will get an exception because the *Print()* method is calling the *PrintMessage()* method over the _service object. Furthermore, if you did not inject anything into the *Service* property, you would not have any object assigned to the _service variable, and the program would not call the *PrintMessage()* over the variable which does not have object state assigned to it.

In the *Main()* method, there is a simple demonstration of this design. In the beginning, there are two objects created, one of *ConfirmationMessageService* class type, and other of the *MessageManager* class type. Notice that the generic constructor is now called for the *MessageManager* object creation. Then, there is the Property Injection, where we assign the *ConfirmationMessageService* object into the *Service* property of the *MessageManager* object. This line puts the value into the private field _service of the *msgManager* variable.

At this moment, everything is ready for calling the *Print()* method over the *msgManager* without any concerns. That is exactly what is done next, and the output will be the message from the *PrintMessage()* method of a *ConfirmationMessageService* class. In the end, we are going to inject another object to demonstrate the second way this program could go. We created a *DeclineMessageService* object and injected it through the *Service* property of the *msgManager* variable. At this moment, we changed the _service field value to have a different object assigned to itself. Now, when executing the *Print()* method, the program will jump to the *PrintMessage()* method of the *DeclineMessageService* class, and it will print the *"Decline injection"* message to the console output. The program output will stay the same as in the previous example, you can check it above.

The last type of dependency injection is the Method Injection, and an example of it is provided below:

```csharp
public interface IService
{
    void PrintMessage();
}
public class ConfirmationMessageService : IService
{
    public void PrintMessage()
    {
        Console.WriteLine("Confirm injection");
    }
}
public class DeclineMessageService : IService
{
    public void PrintMessage()
    {
        Console.WriteLine("Decline injection");
    }
}
public class MessageManager
{
    public void Print(IService service)
    {
        service.PrintMessage();
    }
}

class Program
{
    static void Main(string[] args)
    {
        ConfirmationMessageService msgService = new ConfirmationMessageService();
        MessageManager msgManager = new MessageManager();
        msgManager.Print(msgService);

        DeclineMessageService msgService2 = new DeclineMessageService();
        msgManager.Print(msgService2);
    }
}
```

In this example, the interface component and Service classes remained the same as in the previous two examples. Service classes still implement the *IService* interface. The *PrintMessage()* method of *ConfirmationMessageService* prints the *"Confirm injection"* message, and the *DeclineMessageService* prints the *"Decline injection"* message. Again, the Client class retook its changes, and there was no more private field in which the Service object was stored. There is also no custom constructor, and there are no properties that could implement the dependency injection. Now, there is only one method that will be responsible for the injection. The *Print()* method takes one parameter, and it is an *IService* type object. With that object passed to the method, we are calling the *PrintMessage()* method. This is called Method Injection principle. The method will take an object of some interface type and will call that object's particular method. This is not commonly used, but it is useful when the whole class itself does not require dependency, but only the method holding that dependency. The dependency is injected only for the use of a particular method. Everything is put together in the *Main()* method of a *Program* class once again. There is an instantiation of the *ConfirmationMessageService* object and the *MessageManager* object in the beginning. Then, we run the *Print()* method directly over the *msgManager* object injecting the Service object, which was previously created (the *msgService* variable). This way, the *PrintMessage()* of a *ConfirmationMessageService* class will be called. It will print our well-known message, *"Confirm injection"*. As in the previous examples, we will inject the other class object as well. The *DeclineMessageService* object is created afterward. This object is passed as a parameter to another call of the *Print()* method over the *msgManager* variable object. It is clear that the execution will jump to the *DeclineMessageService* class implementation of the *PrintMessage()* method. This will result in printing the *"Decline injection"* message to the standard output. The console output of this program will look completely the same as in the previous two examples.

Now that you've learned how to implement the dependency injection design pattern, we can successfully move forward to introducing the IoC container, which is also known as dependency injection container. Inversion of Control container represents a framework that is used for the implementation of the automatic dependency injection. Many frameworks can provide this functionality for your software. They are responsible for object instantiation and its period of existence. It is also taking care of injecting the dependencies to a certain class. The IoC container will create an object of the specified class, and it will also inject all of the dependency objects. The injection could possibly happen through a constructor, a property, or a method as we learned until now. This is all happening in the runtime, and the framework is responsible for disposing of the dependencies as well. The advantage of using this container is that we do not have to worry about building and managing the objects manually.

There is a specific lifecycle of the dependency injection container. Each container must provide support for the following three lifecycles in an ongoing way:

1) **Registration** - One of the key things is that the container must provide knowledge about the dependencies that need to be instantiated when the code runs to a certain type. What this means is that the container must find a way to register the mapping of types. This is called registration of the dependencies.

2) **Resolving** - It is already specified that with the IoC, we do not need to instantiate objects manually, and that should be the job of the container. This process in the framework is called resolving. There should be functions that are resolving the provided types. The next process is that the container instantiates the object of a provided type, then injects the needed dependencies, and returns the object as a result.

3) Disposing - Every IoC framework has its own lifetime manager logic, which is taking care of the object's lifecycle and its disposal. This is what every container must provide at the end of the dependency injection usage through the development. The most popular IoC container frameworks that are used in C# are Autofac, Unity, StructureMap, etc. In C#, there is the default dependency injection library. It is stored in the *Microsoft.Extensions.DependencyInjection* namespace. If you do not need complex and fancy things with dependency injection, then this built-in library should be more than enough for you.

One example is provided below:

```
interface ICarManufacturer
{
    void CreateCar();
}

interface ITruckManufacturer
{
    void CreateTruck();
}

class CarManufacturer : ICarManufacturer
{
    public void CreateCar()
    {
        Console.WriteLine("Car Created");
    }
}

class TruckManufacturer : ITruckManufacturer
{
    public void CreateTruck()
    {
        Console.WriteLine("Truck Created");
    }
}
class Program
{
    static void Main(string[] args)
    {
        var serviceProvider = new ServiceCollection()
            .AddSingleton<ICarManufacturer, CarManufacturer>()
            .AddSingleton<ITruckManufacturer, TruckManufacturer>()
            .BuildServiceProvider();

        var carManufacturer = serviceProvider.GetService<ICarManufacturer>();
        carManufacturer.CreateCar();

        var truckManufacturer = serviceProvider.GetService<ITruckManufacturer>();
        truckManufacturer.CreateTruck();
    }
}
```

In this example, we are using the Microsoft Dependency Injection library. There are two defined interface components. One is the *ICarManufacturer*, and the other is the *ITruckManufacturer* interface. The *ICarManufacturer* interface contains one method signature, and that method is *CreateCar()*. Similarly, the *ITruckManufacturer* interface contains one method signature, which is the *CreateTruck()* method. Then, there is a *CarManufacturer* class that implements the *ICarManufacturer* interface. It contains the implementation of the *CreateCar()* method from the interface. This method prints to the console, "Car created" message. We also have a *TruckManufacturer* class exposed. This class implements the *ITruckManufacturer* interface, which means that it contains the implementation of the *CreateTruck()* method. This method prints the *"Truck created"* message to the standard output. The dependency injection occurs in the Main method of the *Program* class. Here, we are creating a *ServiceCollection* object that is used for storing the service objects.

The **AddSingleton()** method adds the CarManufacturer class object for the ICarManufacturer type into the serviceProvider variable. This method adds the element to the serviceProvider collection in a Singleton design pattern way. The Singleton design pattern is something you must also be familiar with, so we will further explain it here. The Singleton design pattern represents the usage of only one object of some type through the application workflow. On the first call to the singleton object, the instantiation is occurring. But each time we call the singleton object, we are only going to get the object that was created after the first call. This means that singleton objects represent the same reference while working with them. The best example of a singleton object could be described with the C# property usage. An example is shown below:

```
private object syncObject = new object();
private List<int> intList;
public List<int> IntList
{
  get
  {
    if(intList == null)
    {
      lock (syncObject)
      {
        if(intList == null)
        {
          intList = new List<int>();
          return intList;
        }
      }
    }
    return intList;
  }
}
```

139

This example is of a thread-safe, read-only singleton implementation. The second null check inside the lock statement guards against the probability that the field gets changed between the first null check and the lock statement. The first null check also keeps the lock statement from executing when it is not necessary, which increases performance by allowing all threads to execute the normal program path without blocking each other. The **lock** statement prevents more than one thread from entering into the protected block of code based off the lock object. The *await* keyword cannot be used inside of a lock statement.

As you can see, whenever the *IntList* property is called in the program, it will always return the same object. The object is created only once, and then it is reused. Now, when the singleton principle is clear, we can continue with the DI example. The *AddSingleton()* method adds the object to the collection in a way that whenever that object is used and pulled out from the collection, it will be the same object, and it will not be created multiple times. When creating the mapping for the *ICarManufacturer* type, the *CarManufacturer* object is used. For the *ITruckManufacturer* type, the *TruckManufacturer* object is used. After the Singleton addings, the *BuildServiceProvider()* method is called, which creates the *ServiceProvider* containing services from the provided collection. This represents the Registration part of the dependency injection. We have registered the mappings of the types and related objects and put them inside a *serviceProvider* collection.

The next thing is the Resolving process. First, we put the *CarManufacturer* object in the *carManufacturer* variable. This object is taken from the *serviceProvider* collection with the *GetService()* method. In the *GetService()* method, we provide the type of object we want to get from the collection. As we provided the *ICarManufacturer*, the *CarManufacturer* class object was returned and stored inside the *carManufacturer* variable. Now we can execute the *CreateCar()* method over the returned object. It will result in printing the *"Car Created"* message onto the console. Then, we also want to take the *TruckManufacturer* object from the *serviceProvider* collection and execute some code with it. We are again using the *GetService()* method, providing the *ITruckManufacturer* type. This will return the *TruckManufacturer* object from the collection, and we will be able to execute the *CreateTruck()* method over that object. It will result in printing the *"Truck Created"* message to the standard output. The output of this program will look like this:

Microsoft Visual Studio Debug Console

```
Car Created
Truck Created

C:\Users\LENOVO\Desktop\EBOOK C#\EBOOK C#\Outline Problem Examples\DependencyInjection\bin\Debug\netcoreapp3.1\Dependenc
yInjection.exe (process 4428) exited with code 0.
To automatically close the console when debugging stops, enable Tools->Options->Debugging->Automatically close the conso
le when debugging stops.
Press any key to close this window . . .
```

8.6 - Object Relational Mappers

The object-relational mapping represents the technique that makes querying the database easier. It allows developers to manipulate the data from the database in an object-oriented approach. The database that is linked with the object-relational mapping technique must be a relational database. The data manipulation from the database without using the ORM can become very unpleasant and complicated because sometimes you must write long and complex SQL queries. Sometimes, developers are not so skilled in working with SQL syntax, and the development process will take more time than needed when it comes to some SQL problems. ORM can enable developers to integrate with the database by only using the programming language in which they are writing the server-side logic. This allows developers to keep their work with SQL at a minimum and to speed up the development process.

ORM simplifies contact with the database by using the objects that are mapped to certain tables from a database. The ORM has one core feature inside its implementation. It is the Data Layer software module. This module represents a library that is responsible for the communication between some object-oriented language and the database. It works as a translator and can handle the data flow that is going on in the middle.

Object-relational mapping is smart enough to provide all CRUD operations from the code. The CRUD operations are well-known database-level operations. The C stands for CREATE; the R stands for READ; the U stands for UPDATE, and the D stands for DELETE. Create inserts the objects as records into some tables. Read selects the data from some tables. Update will update some of the records from a table. Delete erases the record or

141

records from a table. The ORM is perfect for some cases, and not for others. There are pros and cons in every case.

One of the advantages is that the developer has a data model in one place, which makes everything easier to maintain and to stick to the DRY principle (Don't Repeat Yourself). It is also good that you do not have to write poor SQL code, which many of developers do because they do not have appropriate knowledge of it, thereby placing it as a sub-language—which SQL is not, it is a powerful programming language. It's good that ORM uses already-prepared statements for a lot of things; they're easy to call, like whatever method is being called. ORM abstracts the database layer and makes it easily applicable for modifications. It also provides you with the use of object-oriented programming, such as data inheritance. However, there are also disadvantages to using ORM. For example, it is not so good with the performance factor. For large application systems, everything can be slowed down because there are many relations that are not needed in many cases. In that case, SQL master queries are a much safer solution.

Several ORM frameworks are well-supported by C#. The best fit now is probably the **Entity Framework Core ORM**. Let us introduce you more to this popular ORM.

Entity Framework

Entity Framework is the ORM that was released by Microsoft to create the best ORM for C#/.NET applications. The main purpose of the Entity Framework is to make the interaction between C# applications and the relational databases possible. Entity Framework represents a simplifier tool for mapping objects in the code to tables and columns in a particular database. It is important to know that Entity Framework is an open-source tool that is a part of the .NET runtime. So, it can be used free of charge. Entity Framework is responsible for executing the database commands and taking the query results that happen automatically. This ORM can materialize the query results into class objects in C#. The Entity Framework is capable of generating the commands needed to interact with the database in order to read or write data and execute it for you. It has the mechanism to materialize query results into object instances inside your application. You can then access the properties of the objects to get some column values, or you can use LINQ to select a further related object or objects. In the Entity Framework, it is possible to map multiple entities to a single table or map a single entity to multiple database tables. This is the custom mapping functionality that is provided in the Entity Framework.

Microsoft recommends this framework for all new software development processes in C#. The Entity Framework Core represents a model of objects inside the application; it is different from the database model used to persist the application data. The approach is completely different. The model can be aligned with the database schema, but it also can be very different, which provides flexibility. There are two possible approaches to using the Entity Framework Core. The first approach is known as the **Code-First** Approach. In this approach, you must create classes inside the code that will represent the tables in the database. When classes and their properties are created, you can execute the command to update the database schema. At this moment, the database will be changed to create or update the tables that are mapped to the classes inside the code. The other approach is the **Database-First** approach. In this approach, the opposite thing is done. First, we must create or update the database schema through SQL, or any tool capable of doing it. After the database schema is changed, we can execute the command to create or update the class models inside the application code, which will be mapped to the tables from the database. Whatever matches your requirements and application design can be chosen.

We will now present an example of Entity Framework Core ORM usage:

```
5 references
public class Car
{
    0 references
    public int Id { get; set; }
    5 references
    public string Make { get; set; }
    6 references
    public string Model { get; set; }
    5 references
    public int Year { get; set; }
    4 references
    public bool IsTurboCharged { get; set; }
}

5 references
class CarContext : DbContext
{
    0 references
    public CarContext() { }
    1 reference
    public CarContext(DbContextOptions<CarContext> options) : base(options) { }

    5 references
    public DbSet<Car> Cars { get; set; }

    2 references
    protected override void OnConfiguring(DbContextOptionsBuilder optionsBuilder)
    {
        if (!optionsBuilder.IsConfigured)
        {
            throw new Exception("Must pass optionsBuilder in for use");
        }
    }
}
```

In this example, we will demonstrate a program that uses the Entity Framework Core object-relational mapper. Here, you can see a class model named *Car*. The *Car* class has a few properties, and each of them will represent one column in the *Car* table, which will be created in the in-memory simulated database for this example. The properties that will be mapped to columns are *Id*, *Make*, *Model*, *Year*, and *IsTurboCharged*. In order to create a database, we will need some database context. In the second class, we are creating a component that will be responsible for the database context. A *CarContext* class will inherit from the *DbContext* class, which is the Entity Framework Core built-in class. In the constructor of the *CarContext*, we pass the *DbContextOptions* object of the *CarContext* type. This object is forwarded to the base constructor, which means that it forwards to the generic *DbContext* class constructor. We must also declare a *DbSet* of *Car* objects. In this *DbSet* variable, all entities (records from the database) of *Car* objects will be stored. Those objects will represent the records from the database in the *Car* table. There is also one method that should be overridden, and that is the *OnConfiguring()* method from the *DbContext* class. This method does not have an implementation in its core class. In order to configure the database, we must override this method and implement it. This method is called for every instance of the database context creation. We will just check here if it is the options builder configured for the database. If it is not, we will throw an exception. Now, we are ready to create the database and to execute some database-level commands.

```
class Program
{
    static void Main(string[] args)
    {
        var options = new DbContextOptionsBuilder<CarContext>()
            .UseInMemoryDatabase(databaseName: "CarsDatabase")
            .Options;

        using (var context = new CarContext(options))
        {
            context.Cars.Add(new Car()
            {
                IsTurboCharged = false,
                Make = "Toyota",
                Model = "Corolla",
                Year = 2019
            });

            context.Cars.Add(new Car()
            {
                IsTurboCharged = true,
                Make = "Honda",
                Model = "Civic",
                Year = 2017
            });

            context.Cars.Add(new Car()
            {
                IsTurboCharged = false,
                Make = "Ford",
                Model = "Model-T",
                Year = 1908
            });

            context.Cars.Add(new Car()
            {
                IsTurboCharged = false,
                Make = "Dodge",
                Model = "Viper",
                Year = 1998
            });

            context.SaveChanges();
            var car = context.Cars.FirstOrDefault(s => s.Model == "Viper");
            Console.WriteLine($"You retrieved the {car.Year} {car.Make}
{car.Model}");
        }
    }
}
```

In the *Main()* method of the *Program* class, the first thing that will be done is the creation of the in-memory database, whose name is *CarsDatabase*. The creation of the database is done, and the Options property is taken from the *DbContextOptionsBuilder* and stored into the **options** variable. Now we are ready to play with the database through the Entity Framework Core commands. In the **using** statement, we will manipulate the data and do some insertions and retrieval. To understand the using statement, you must first learn what the **try-catch** block is. During programming, many

145

errors can occur in the program, but when this happens, C# throws an exception, and the program will stop the execution. That is not great for the user experience, so when the error happens, we must find a way to process it correctly and let the program continue the execution without stopping. This is realized in the *try-catch* block.

In the *try* block, we should insert the code that has the possibility to throw an exception. If the exception is thrown, then the program will jump into the *catch* block, allowing us to take control of the exception, and possibly print the error message to the user, and continue the execution without stopping. In the *try-catch* block, there is also one more block that could be implemented. It is the **finally** block.

The *finally* block comes under the *catch* block, and it represents code that will be executed regardless of whether the exception happened or not. So, we are implementing the *finally* block when we want to do something right after the main execution in the *try* block, or after the error is thrown. The **using** statement represents the shorter version of the *try-catch* block. In the *using* statement, there is a built-in *try-catch* block, and if the exception happens, it will be processed automatically in the *using* statement. The *using* statement will call the *Dispose()* method after the code block execution even if the code throws an exception. So, here we are initializing the *CarContext*, passing the options object to the instantiation of the **context** object. After that, we access the virtual *Car* table from the database by using the **context.Cars** database set. As mentioned earlier, this database set represents the *Car* table with its records (objects). So, we are using the **Add()** method to add four different objects into the set. These objects will represent records in the table. It is important to know that the objects are not saved in the database when using the **Add** method. They are just locally added. Every change done over the context is done just locally until the *SaveChanges()* method is called on the database context object. After the objects are added to the database set, we then performed the *SaveChanges()* method, and at that moment, all new objects that have been added to the database set are inserted into the database.

Now, we are able to retrieve some data from the database. We will do this again with the Entity Framework Core, accessing the database context, and *Cars* database set. There is a need to retrieve the Car object that has a *Model* name equal to *"Viper"*. This can be done with the help of LINQ. We will access the database set, and then we will be able to perform filtering with the LINQ query. We will then use the *FirstOrDefault()* LINQ method to retrieve the required information. The *FirstOrDefault()* method finds the first occurrence of the object if there is a match and returns its value. If there is no match for the specified filter, this method will return the default value of the type searched. For example, in this case, if there is no car object with the *"Viper"* value in the *Model* column, the null value will be returned. But we are yet happy to have that object, and this method will get the desired information successfully. The object is stored in the **car** variable, and then, accessing its properties, we will print the *Year*, *Make*, and *Model* of the selected car to the console output. The result of this program would look like this:

8.7 - Mappers

In this chapter, you will learn what mappers are, why we use them, and how to implement them. While working as a software developer, you are constantly in need of manipulating objects. Since objects are used all the time in the object-oriented programming principle, developers always struggle with some object changes, modifications, instantiations, etc. In some cases, frequent nowadays, there is a need for data mapping between two objects. When some values are required to transfer from one object to another, it is called object-mapping.

The most common situation where we need object mapping is when working in Web API projects. The web applications today are mostly Web API applications with one client-side application, which represents some frontend framework (for example, Angular or React) that is connected with a particular backend application. The communication between frontend and backend happens most of the time. In that communication, many objects are transferred from frontend to backend and vice versa. The typical example would be when there is a form on the frontend from which field values must be packed to a certain object and transferred to the backend. This transferred object is required to be saved as a record inside the particular table in the database. If, for example, the backend application is using an ORM like the Entity

147

Framework Core, then the object that came from the frontend must be mapped to the model object.

As we learned in the ORM chapter, the model object represents the record from a particular table. In this case, the transferred object should be mapped to the model object, and then, the model object should be saved over the database context. The other frequent example would be the data transferred in the opposite direction. Imagine there is a page inside the frontend application that represents the information about some business model objects. When you land on that page, the client-side application then sends a request to get the information about the wanted object. On the backend side, you have to retrieve the object from the database table, and have it stored in the model object of the Entity Framework Core ORM. Then, that model object must be mapped to the frontend class type object and transferred through the protocol back in the client-side application, where the pieces of information will be shown to the user. These are the most common data mapping actions that are being resolved in web applications nowadays.

Object mappings can be done manually, mappers can be custom created, but it would take time. Due to this, many applications use already built mapper libraries that can support various mappings between objects. In C#, the best-suited mapper library is probably the AutoMapper. It is a free library that can be used in any C# application. The AutoMapper can save a lot of time and effort that you would have lost while trying to map properties manually each time you needed object mapping.

Come on now, let's check out one AutoMapper usage example:

```
internal class EuropeanCar
{
    public bool IsAutomatic { get; set; }
    public string Make { get; set; }
    public string Model { get; set; }
    public int Year { get; set; }
    public string DriverSide { get; set; }
}

internal class AmericanCar
{
    public bool IsAutomatic { get; set; }
    public string Make { get; set; }
    public string Model { get; set; }
    public int Year { get; set; }
    public string DriverSide { get; set; }
}
```

In the beginning, there are two classes exposed. As you may assume, the objects of those two classes are the ones that will be mapped. The first class is called *EuropeanCar*, and the second class is called *AmericanCar*. The AutoMapper works in the following way: it scans the property names for both classes that are supposed to be mapped. For the property names that are matched in both classes, it will do the automatic value transfer from one object property to another. So, in conclusion, when you are using the AutoMapper, the classes of the objects that you want to map must have the same property names. If they do not have the same names, the mapping will be executed only on the properties that are matched by name. The properties that are not matched by name will have their default type values in the mapped object. Now, let's see how we will put this together:

```
class Program
{
    static void Main(string[] args)
    {
        var config = new MapperConfiguration(configuration =>
        {
            configuration.CreateMap<EuropeanCar, AmericanCar>()
                .ForMember(x => x.DriverSide,
                    opt =>
                        opt.MapFrom( o => "Left"));
        });

        IMapper mapper = config.CreateMapper();

        EuropeanCar europeanCar = new EuropeanCar()
        {
            Year = 2019,
            Make = "Toyota",
            Model = "Corolla",
            IsAutomatic = true,
            DriverSide = "Right"
        };

        AmericanCar americanCar = mapper.Map<EuropeanCar, AmericanCar>(europeanCar);

        Console.WriteLine($"The American version of the car has the driver on the
{americanCar.DriverSide}");
    }
}
```

Here, we will demonstrate the mappings of the objects from the previously explained classes. The first thing that must be done is the creation of the *MappingConfiguration* object from the AutoMapper library. When creating this configuration, we must provide the mappings and all the details needed for the mappings. In this case, we are creating only one map definition, and that is the mapping of the *EuropeanCar* class object to the *AmericanCar* class object. The *CreateMap()* method is creating the definition for assigning property values from the *EuropeanCar* object to the *AmericanCar* object. Everything after the *CreateMap()* method call represents certain definitions for the custom and additional logic of mapping properties. In this case, there is one custom mapping for the *DriverSide* property. In the *ForMember()* method, we are defining a custom map for a certain property; in this case, every *DriverSide* value from the *EuropeanCar* class will be mapped differently to the *AmericanCar* object. In the AmericanCar object, the *DriverSide* property value will always be mapped as the *"Left"* string value. So, whatever comes from the source object, the value of the *DriverSide* in the destination object will be the string *"Left"*.

After the generic and custom mapping definitions are created, we are ready to instantiate the *IMapper* type object over which we call the mapping methods. Next, we create an object of the *EuropeanCar* class type. This object will be used for the mapping and the creation of the *AmericanCar* object through the AutoMapper. The *Map()* method is executed over the mapper object, and the new instance of the *AmericanCar* class is created. The *Map()* method has many overloads, but in this case, it is required to provide the source object type first and the destination object type second, after which there is a concrete source object passed to the function. This will create a new instance of the AmericanCar class inside AutoMapper, and all properties will be mapped as defined in the configuration. After the creation and mapping are done, the *Map()* method then returns the newly created object of the destination type class. Now, in the *AmericanCar* variable, we have the complete object with all of the property values mapped from the source object. In the end, we want to print the custom mapped property in order to check if everything went well in the AutoMapper. The program output will look like this:

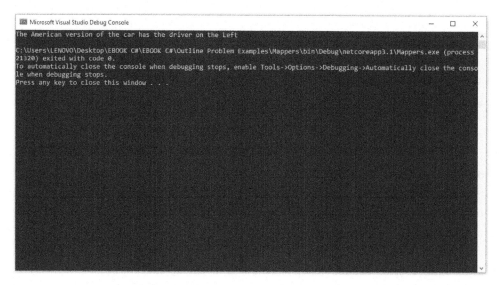

The program printed the correct and expected behavior. The mapping for the *AmericanCar* property *DriverSide* is *"Left"*, which we have defined in the configuration of the mappings. Additionally, you can try to print out the other property values from the *americanCar* variable, and you will see that all the values are the same as from the source object *europeanCar*. AutoMapper is a powerful tool, isn't it?

150

8.8 - Unit Testing

Unit testing represents a principle of testing the particular software unit or module in order to define that it's ready for usage and to see if the functionality behaves well. Unit testing is, in fact, automated tests that are developed and run by developers. It is supposed to assure that the unit or any application section is working as expected and that it matches the design and correct behavior. Unit testing can be performed on both procedural and object-oriented programming. From the code aspect, a unit test can be the entire module of the application; it can be an individual method, an entire class functionality, certain application flow through the multiple method executions, etc. The best way is to write tests for the smallest testable units, build, and proceed with more complex tests that are combining the smallest units together into some logical code execution flow. While programming software, developers should create the criteria and the results which are detected as correct behavior and insert them into tests to verify the exactness of the tested component. What is required to achieve is the isolation of every small part of the application and proving that those individual sections are working correctly. The advantages of writing unit tests while developing software are multitude. Unit tests are always there to discover the problems inside the software in their early phases. The development cycle is often to last longer if unit tests are included for every functionality. It prolongs the time of completion, but it improves the quality of software that will be delivered. The unit test can detect bugs in implementation, as well as some missing logical parts of the component tested. If the developer knows that he must write a unit test for the functionality that he is developing, it forces him to think more sharply, and it also produces better and higher quality code. The developer then thinks more about input cases, potential outputs, potential errors, which will make you code better and write high-quality tested code. The significance of finding problems in the code in the early development cycle is crucial. It could reduce the enormous amount of time. The cost of finding potential problems early is very low, unlike the cost of identifying, debugging and correcting bugs later in the development cycle. Poor code quality can stop you from creating unit tests because it can become impossible to test the particular unit if it is coded at a low-quality level. This is why test-driven development is forcing programmers to analyze better, structuring the classes and methods in a better way. If not found, the problems can be released for the client's live usage of the application, which could lead to various problems in the future. The use of unit testing is making a developer able to refactor every code part if needed, yet ensure that the application component is still working as expected. A best practice is to create test cases for all methods and working flows. This way, whenever some change in the code creates a bug, it could be identified very fast.

When following test-driven development, commonly known as **TDD**, unit tests are supposed to be written before the code functionality itself. When the unit test is done, and the feature is also done, the developer should run the test and check whether the functionality works correctly. If the test passes, the feature is considered to be complete and accurate. Unit tests are supposed to run while the development process is not finished. If the test passed today, it doesn't mean it's going to pass tomorrow. There is a chance that new functionality or some code that is related to an already tested functionality could break the test that was marked as good. This is why tests are run in a loop until the whole development is finished. If some test execution fails, it is considered that there is a problem in a feature or a problem in a test. Sometimes tests must be changed, and some things should be added in order to cover the correct behavior. When a test fails, it does not always mean that the feature is not correct; the test can also be the reason for failure. Test-driven development helps to identify the problems before handling the functionality to testers or clients. It reduces the chance of something being missed or badly provided.

Besides the numerous advantages that unit testing usage contains, there are also some limitations and disadvantages, like for almost every approach in computer programming. Unit tests are not always certain to detect every problem and bug in the software because it cannot cover every execution flow. Unit tests are supposed to catch errors only in some small targeted places inside the code. They also don't catch performance issues of the functionality. So, the conclusion is that unit tests cannot prove the complete absence of errors, but still, they can be very helpful. It is not possible to know all possible inputs for some functionality, as by definition, the unit testing principle only covers the testing of small units. However, there are also other testing approaches that are supposed to track and identify problems not in a single unit, but in some flow, or whole execution path. This approach is called **integration testing**. There are also a few more testing approaches that are helpful to achieve software quality, such as penetration testing, User Interface (UI) automated testing, etc. When a method has known input parameters and a certain output, in that case, unit tests tend to be the most comfortable. On the other hand, it's not easy to write a unit test when some functions are interacting with external components outside the application, such as web services, databases, etc. For example, if the method is calling some web service, and the result of the call is used for some purpose further in the method, then the developer must mock the service response. The service responses could be multiple, so in that case, the developer will have a problem because he would need to cover every possible response type of the external web service. There is also a problem when the method is working closely with the database. In that case, the developer must create a mockup of the database or the database section (some table records or similar), which is very likely not to be as good as the real database, and the real database interactions.

A mockup, in the context of testing, is an imitation database, class, method, etc. that replaces or stands in for the real item to make testing easier.

Now, let us talk more about the testing approach that correlates closely to the unit testing. This testing principle is **integration testing**. Integration testing represents a software testing paradigm where individual components are linked and tested as a group. The focus inside this principle is to find problems between interactions of the smallest units. The smallest units are supposed to be tested in unit tests, and their relations, connections, and dependencies are to be tested inside integration tests. In the integration testing principle, there are several approaches. The Big-Bang approach is when all of the units are combined and tested at once. The Top-Down approach to integration testing is when top-level units are tested at the beginning, and lower-level units are tested after that, in a respective way. The bottom-up testing approach to integration testing is the opposite of the Top-Down approach. So, it is when low-level units are tested first, and the upper-level units are tested afterwards. The last approach is the Sandwich or the Hybrid approach. It represents the combination of the Bottom-up and Top-down integration testing approaches. There are a few things that are required for integration testing success. The developer should ensure that there is proper design information where all of the possible interactions between units are described. It is not possible to execute integration testing without this information clearly defined. The developer should be sure that each unit is tested separately before putting them into an integration test. If the units are not covered correctly with their own usage tests, the integration tests would not have any sense because they would be performed with the badly tested smaller units. Developers must automate their tests, especially when using the top-down, bottom-up, or hybrid approach. This is because the regression testing will be re-executed each time a unit is inserted into an integration test.

For unit testing in C#, there are a few frameworks that support it. They have implementation for the creation of a unit test, initial setup values, and all the logic of the unit test execution. The most popular that are used often in C# are NUnit and XUnit frameworks. The Visual Studio contains some built-in unit testing tool that is also commonly used. All of the testing frameworks are here to suggest the same goal at the end. They support developers to write unit tests faster, easier, and much simpler than without using the framework. The unit testing frameworks offer almost all similar features, but they surely differ between each other. Some frameworks are concentrated just on the execution of very complex tests, while other frameworks are focused more on usability and simplicity of writing and executing the tests. The frameworks have differences, and they all group the priorities by their judgment, but at the end of the day, they all serve the same final goal.

This goal is to define a clear path for a developer for the creation, execution, performance, and stability of the unit tests. Now, we will demonstrate the whole process of a few small unit tests. We will test the code and provide the results to familiarize you with the paradigm.

For this explanation, we have chosen the NUnit framework for unit testing. We have created one NUnit test project inside our solution in Visual Studio. This project will contain references from the other projects inside our solution, which we will provide to it. Every project reference that has certain units that need to be tested will be inserted into the test project. This allows the unit test project to access the desired part of the code from other projects. For this example, we have created a new project where we will test the code for unit tests. This project name is called *TestableProject*. Inside this project, we have added one class named *UnitTestsExample* as shown below:

```csharp
public class UnitTestsExample
{
    0 references
    public bool GreaterThan(int a, int b)
    {
        return (a > b);
    }

    0 references
    public bool ContainsText(string text, string substring)
    {
        return text.Contains(substring);
    }

    0 references
    public int FindElementIndex(List<int> array, int elem)
    {
        for (int i = 0; i < array.Count; i++)
        {
            if (array[i] == elem)
            {
                return 1;
            }
        }

        return -1;
    }

    0 references
    public string KeyValue(int key)
    {
        switch (key)
        {
            case 0:
                return "Zero";
            case 1:
                return "One";
            case 2:
                return "Two";
            case 3:
                return "Three";
            case 4:
                return "Four";
            case 5:
                return "Five";
            default:
                return "NoValue";
        }
    }
}
```

Here, we have exposed one class named *UnitTestsExample*, which will be fully tested inside our NUnit *TestProject*. This class contains four public methods. The first method is the *GreaterThan()* method. This method returns *bool* value as a result. It takes two parameters, and both are *int* values. The logic is simple. If the first parameter passed is greater than the second, the method will return true as a result to the caller thread. If the second parameter value is greater than the first, the method will return a false value.

The second method is the *ContainsText()* method. This method also returns the bool type as a result. It takes two parameters, the first one is the string text, and the second one is the string *substring*. With this method, we will determine whether the text contains passed substring inside of it. For this, we will use the *Contains()* string extension method. This method will conclude if the text does contain a substring. If yes, the method will return a true value; if not, the result will be *false*.

The third method inside this class is the *FindElementIndex()* method. This method returns *int* as a result of the execution. It takes two arguments, the first one is the List of *int* values, and the second argument is the *int* value which will be searched inside the previously passed *List<int>*. This will be done inside the *for* loop statement. We will create one counter variable that will represent the index of the *List<int>* element. In every iteration, the program will increment the counter by one. Inside the body code block of the loop, there is a check to see if the element on the current index is equal to the passed element value. If equality is found, the index of the found element inside the array is returned as a result of this method. If no element equal to the passed value is found inside the array variable, the method will return -1 as a result.

The last method inside this class is the *KeyValue()* method. This is a public method that returns the string type as a result of the execution. It takes one parameter that represents the key *int* value. Inside the switch statement, there is logic that checks to see if the passed value is any number between zero and five. There are six elements inside the switch statement, for each key between numbers zero and five, the string representation of the number will be returned. If the passed key is not any of the numbers from zero to five, the method returns the generic message *"NoValue"*, which indicates that there is no corresponding string representation within this method for the passed number parameter.

Now that we have the class, we can review the testing of this small programming unit:

```csharp
public class Tests
{
    UnitTestsExample instance;

    [SetUp]
    public void Setup()
    {
        instance = new UnitTestsExample();
    }

    [Test]
    public void GreaterThanTest()
    {
        bool greaterThan = instance.GreaterThan(5, 4);
        Assert.AreEqual(true, greaterThan);
    }

    [Test]
    public void ContainsTextTest()
    {
        bool containsText = instance.ContainsText("New text", "Old");
        Assert.AreEqual(false, containsText);

        containsText = instance.ContainsText("New text", "New");
        Assert.AreEqual(true, containsText);
    }

    [Test]
    public void FindIndexTest()
    {
        List<int> newlist = new List<int>
        {
            1,5,6,3,8,22,45
        };

        var index = instance.FindElementIndex(newlist, 22);
        Assert.AreEqual(5, index);
    }

    [Test]
    public void KeyValueTest()
    {
        var result = instance.KeyValue(6);
        Assert.AreEqual("Six", result);
    }
}
```

Here you can see one Test class from the NUnit test project. Inside this class, we will test the code from the *UnitTestsExample* class. As you can see, there are several public void methods inside this Test class. Above each of them, there is an attribute defined inside the *[ ]* characters. The first one you will see is the *[SetUp]* attribute above the *Setup()* method. This attribute means that the NUnit framework will execute this method first when a test or tests are run. Inside this method, we should always put some initial values and things that we want to declare and use throughout the tests. Above this method, there is a declaration of the instance variable of a UnitTestsExample class type. This object gets instantiated inside the *Setup()* method. This will be executed first, and this object will be used in every test below the Setup method.

The first unit test is *GreaterThanTest*. We are calling the *GreaterThan()* method over the instance object and store the result inside the *greaterThan bool* variable. This method is called with the *5* and *4* parameter values, which means that we are expecting the *true* value to be returned, *5* is greater than *4* obviously. The NUnit framework uses the Assert class to check the correctness. Inside this class, there are many methods that check the accuracy of the code results in many different ways. In this example, we will use the *AreEqual()* method, which takes two objects and checks their equality. Since *5* is greater than *4*, we assume that the true value is the expected value, and as the second parameter to the *AreEqual()* method, we are sending the result of the *GreaterThan()* execution.

The second unit test inside this example is the *ContainsTextTest*. We will call the *ContainsText()* method over the instance object with the *"New text"* and *"Old"* strings passed in arguments. So, we are trying to determine if the string *"Old"* is a substring of the "New text." The result of the execution is stored in the *containsText* variable. The expected condition is false, and it is compared with the result stored in the *containsText* variable. This should be marked as passed because *"Old"* is not contained inside the *"New text"* string. Then we will try the same thing, but with different parameters that should provide a true result with the substring comparison. Those parameters are now *"New text"* and *"New"*. This should also pass because the expected value is now set to true, and the method execution should also return true because *"New"* is contained inside the *"New text"* string.

The next unit test is the *FindIndexTest()* method. We have created one list with seven values. After this, the program is calling the *FindElementIndex()* method over the instance object passing the previously instantiated *List<int>* object and the value *22* for search. The result of this execution will be stored inside the index variable. Finally, we are doing the *Assert* with the *AreEqual()* method, passing *5* as the expected index (because number *22* is at index *5* inside the created list) and the index variable value. This should result in a passed test.

The last test is *KeyValueTest*. We are testing the *KeyValue()* method of the *UnitTestsExample* class. The program is trying to find the string representation of number *6*, which is passed as a parameter to the method execution. The outcome is stored in the result variable. Then we are checking the result value by assuming that the expected value should be string *"Six"*. This assertion will not pass because, in the *KeyValue()* method implementation, there are cases from zero to five. All other numbers will result in the generic message *"NoValue"*.

Now we will run those tests and check for the final outcome.

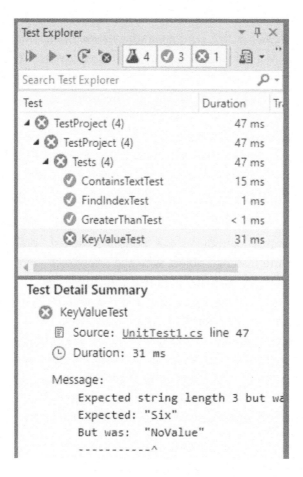

Here, in the Test Explorer in the Visual Studio editor, you can see all of the tests we have created. As expected, the first three tests passed, but the last test failed. You can also see the detailed summary of the failed test.

Chapter 9: The Final Project

Congratulations, you have completed all the chapters about C# programming language. We saved the best for the end. We've created a small interactive application in which we've shown all the techniques and important things about C# combined. You'll be able to see almost everything you've learned so far and pack everything together in a small, but functional software solution. This is the interactive console application in which there are user interactions and program response. It is about a small Car Dealership functioning. We will start from the files and folders organized inside the application. Every application should have well-organized resource storage, so that developers can easily manage everything. The app folder tree looks like this:

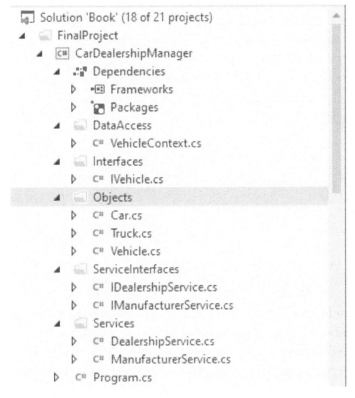

In the above picture, you can see a well-organized small application structure. The name of the project is *CarDealershipManager*. Inside this solution, the first thing you will see are the dependencies. In the dependencies folder, there are always some pulled-in frameworks and references, such as .NET Core framework library.

Inside the packages folder, there are external libraries and other sources that are included inside our application, and we need them for certain things. The examples of those packages are Entity Framework Core, Dependency Injection support, etc. Below that, you can see folder structuring. There is a *DataAccess* folder that contains one class that will represent everything about database context. This folder is the data layer of our application. Inside this folder, there will be everything related to the configuration and management of the database. The next folder is the Interfaces folder, where we will store our interface components for the application. Here we have only one interface component—*IVehicle* interface.

The next folder is the *Objects* folder. Inside this folder, there are classes of the entities, which will be required for data manipulation. You can see three classes here: *Car*, *Truck*, and the *Vehicle* class. The next folder is the *ServiceInterfaces* folder. Here we have the interface component, which will be responsible for the dependency injection of the service objects. Each of these interfaces will have one class that implements it. The final folder is the *Services* folder. As you've probably already noticed, these are the service classes that will implement the interfaces from the previous folder. These service classes will be used for the dependency injection. In the end, there is a Program.cs file that contains one *Program* class with its *Main()* method. As we have learned until now, inside this method, everything will be put together and made to work precisely. Now, let's break this into sections and explain it part by part. First, we will start with the *Objects* folder and its logic:

```
interface IVehicle
{
    bool IsAutomatic { get;}
    string Vin { get; }
}
```

Before the class implementation, we inserted the code from the only interface component that is inside the Interfaces folder. This interface has two read-only properties, and its name is *IVehicle*. The properties are boolean *IsAutomatic* and string *Vin*. Below the interface component, we have exposed the code from each of the three classes inside the *Objects* folder. The first class is the *Vehicle* class. This class is implementing the *IVehicle* interface, which means that it will have the implementation of the two properties inside the *IVehicle*. Besides those two properties, it contains the *Id* property of the *int* data type. The properties *IsAutomatic* and *Vin* have the *set* visibility set to *protected*, and this means that those properties could be a value-assigned inside parent and inherited class. After the property definitions, there is a *Vehicle* constructor, which takes two parameters and assigns their values to the *IsAutomatic* and *Vin* property, respectively.

```csharp
class Vehicle:IVehicle
{
    0 references
    public int Id { get; set; }
    6 references
    public bool IsAutomatic { get; protected set; }
    12 references
    public string Vin { get; protected set; }

    2 references
    public Vehicle(bool isAutomatic, string vin)
    {
        IsAutomatic = isAutomatic;
        Vin = vin;
    }
}

class Car:Vehicle
{
    3 references
    public int TrunkSpace { get; }

    2 references
    public Car(bool isAutomatic, string vin, int trunkSpace) : base(isAutomatic,vin)
    {
        if (trunkSpace > 500)
        {
            throw new Exception("Trunk space for a car cannot exceed 500");
        }

        TrunkSpace = trunkSpace;
    }
}


class Truck:Vehicle
{
    3 references
    public int BedSpace { get; }
    2 references
    public Truck(bool isAutomatic, string vin,int bedSpace) : base(isAutomatic,vin)
    {
        if (bedSpace < 500)
        {
            throw new Exception("Bed space for a truck cannot be below 500");
        }

        BedSpace = bedSpace;
    }
}
```

161

The next class is the *Car* class. This class inherits the *Vehicle* class—so the *Vehicle* class is the parent class of the *Car* class. It can access all the properties from the *Vehicle* class, and it also has its own property. The *Car* property is the *TrunkSpace* read-only property. The *Car's* own constructor uses three parameters, the values for the *IsAutomatic* property, the *Vin* property, and the *TrunkSpace* property. This constructor passes the parent property values from the parameter to the base constructor. It means that it called the base constructor with the *isAutomatic* and *vin* parameter values passed. In the implementation of its own constructor, there is a check on whether the *trunkSpace* parameter value is greater than five hundred. If the condition is true, the program will throw an exception with the message *"Trunk space for a car cannot exceed 500"*. Below the condition check, there is a classic property initial state assignment of the *TrunkSpace* property.

The last class is the *Truck* class, which also inherits from the *Vehicle* class. We can assume that the *Truck* and *Car* are the child classes of the *Vehicle* class. It has one read-only property named *BedSpace*. In the constructor of a *Truck* class, there is a similar thing as in the *Car* constructor. Three parameters are passed from which two of them are furthered to the base class constructor, and those are *isAutomatic* and *vin* parameter values. In the body of its own constructor, there is a check to see if the *bedSpace* parameter value is less than five hundred. Similarly, like in the *Car* class, if the condition is *true*, the program will throw an exception with the message *"Bed space for a truck cannot be below 500"*. After that, there is a common property state assignment of the *BedSpace* read-only property.

The next thing to be explained is the *DataLayer*, which, in this case, represents the *VehicleContext* class. Let's take a look at the code:

```
class VehicleContext:DbContext
{
    public VehicleContext(){ }
    public VehicleContext(DbContextOptions<VehicleContext> options) : base(options){ }
    public DbSet<Vehicle> Vehicles { get; set; }
    public DbSet<Car> Cars { get; set; }
    public DbSet<Truck> Trucks { get; set; }

    protected override void OnConfiguring(DbContextOptionsBuilder optionsBuilder)
    {
        if (!optionsBuilder.IsConfigured)
        {
            throw new Exception("Must pass optionsBuilder in for use");
        }
    }

    protected override void OnModelCreating(ModelBuilder modelBuilder)
    {
        modelBuilder.Entity<Car>()
            .Property(b => b.TrunkSpace).ValueGeneratedNever();
        modelBuilder.Entity<Car>()
            .Property(b => b.Vin).ValueGeneratedNever();
        modelBuilder.Entity<Car>()
            .Property(b => b.IsAutomatic).ValueGeneratedNever();

        modelBuilder.Entity<Truck>()
            .Property(b => b.BedSpace).ValueGeneratedNever();
        modelBuilder.Entity<Truck>()
            .Property(b => b.Vin).ValueGeneratedNever();
        modelBuilder.Entity<Truck>()
            .Property(b => b.IsAutomatic).ValueGeneratedNever();
        base.OnModelCreating(modelBuilder);
    }
}
```

This is a data layer class. The *VehicleContext* class is extending the *DbContext* class from Entity Framework Core package. In this class, we can see two public constructors. The first one is an empty constructor that creates the instance of the *VehicleContext* without any initial state assigned. The second constructor takes one parameter of the *DbContextOptions<VehicleContext>* object. This constructor does not also have its own implementation. Still, it is passing the *DbContextOptions<VehicleContext>* object to its base constructor in the *DbContext* class to assign the options for the context. This constructor forces the Entity Framework Core to do the context initialization instead of us. After the constructors, there are three *DbSet* properties. Each of them will represent the table content from a database. The first one will be a *Vehicle* database set, the second and third one—its children, *Car* and *Truck* database sets. Then, there is a standard override of the *OnConfiguring()* method from the *DbContext* class. Here, we are just checking to see if the *DbContextOptionsBuilder* object is configured. If it is not configured, we will throw an exception with the message of *"Must pass optionsBuilder in for use"*.

The last thing in this class is the override of the *OnModelCreating()* method from the *DbContext* class. This method is setting the fluent configuration for the model properties, and adds additional bindings and logic for database actions to work if it is needed. This method has one parameter passed, and it is a *ModelBuilder* class object that is responsible for managing the fluent configuration of the entities. In this overridden implementation, there is a *ValueGeneratedNever()* method executed over each property from the *Car* and the *Truck* model objects. This means that each of these properties will never have a generated value by the database when the instance of their entities are saved. So, for all three properties of the *Car* model and the *Truck* model, the values will never be generated from the database side when the record is saved to the database. After this execution, there is a call to the *OnModelCreating()* method from the base class in order to configure the generic fluent database work. This was all about the data layer class from our car dealership application. We can now move on to the dependency injection-based components:

```
interface IDealershipService
{
    List<IVehicle> GetInventory();
    IVehicle GetVehicle(string vin);
    void SellVehicle(string vin);
    void AddVehicleToInventory(IVehicle vehicle);
}

interface IManufacturerService
{
    IVehicle BuyVehicle();
}
```

The *ServiceInterfaces* folder is next to be detailed. Inside that folder, we have two service interface components, shown above, that will be implemented by the service classes in order to achieve dependency injection. The first interface component is the *IDealershipService*. This interface is the dealership-oriented interface, and it has signatures of four methods:

1) The *GetInventory()* method, which will return the List of *IVehicle* type objects in the implementation.
2) The *GetVehicle()* method, which has one parameter—the vehicle identification number, based on the method we will use to return the *IVehicle* type object to the caller.
3) Then, the *SellVehicle()* method, which will obviously remove the vehicle from a certain inventory base on the vehicle identification number, passed as a parameter.
4) Lastly, the *AddVehicleToInventory()* method with the *IVehicle* type object in the argument will add the object to the inventory list.

The second interface is simpler, and it has only one method. The *IManufacturerService* interface component has only the *BuyVehicle()* method, which returns the *IVehicle* type object. It is a manufacturer-based interface.

Those were the service interface components that are ready to be implemented by the service classes. Now, we can go ahead and check the service classes, their implementation, and logic.

```
class DealershipService:IDealershipService
{
    private VehicleContext _vehicleContext;

    public DealershipService(VehicleContext vehicleContext)
    {
        _vehicleContext = vehicleContext;
    }

    public List<IVehicle> GetInventory()
    {
        List<IVehicle> vehicles = new List<IVehicle>();

        vehicles.AddRange(_vehicleContext.Cars);
        vehicles.AddRange(_vehicleContext.Trucks);

        return vehicles;
    }
}
```

The first service class that will be explained is the *DealershipService* class. The code of this class will be split into a few parts, and each part will be separately explained because of the size of the class. The *DealershipService* class implements the *IDealershipService* interface component, and it will implement all of the methods from this interface. The first thing in this class that you can notice is the private field *_vehicleContext*, which is of *VehicleContext* class type. This field's state will be set in the class constructor, as provided above. The first method that is implemented is the *GetInventory()* method. This method is supposed to return the *List* of *IVehicle* objects. In the beginning, we are instantiating *List<IVehicle>* type object. This object is empty in the beginning. Then, the list is populated by the *Cars* and *Trucks* lists from the given context. This means that we are adding all of the *Car* objects and all of the *Truck* objects from the *_vehicleContext*. The *Cars* and *Trucks* properties inside the context object are representing the records from the *Car* and *Truck* table in the database. It means that the list which we will return as a result of this method execution will have all of the objects from the *Truck* and *Car* database tables. After we added those two database sets into our list, we return it as a result to the caller of the method. Now we can move forward with the explanation of the next methods:

```
public IVehicle GetVehicle(string vin)
{
    IVehicle vehicle;
    vehicle = _vehicleContext.Cars.FirstOrDefault(s => s.Vin == vin);

    if (vehicle == null)
    {
        vehicle = _vehicleContext.Trucks.FirstOrDefault(s => s.Vin == vin);
    }

    if (vehicle == null)
    {
        throw new Exception($"Vehicle does not exist with VIN {vin}");
    }

    return vehicle;
}
public void SellVehicle(string vin)
{
    IVehicle vehicle;
    vehicle = _vehicleContext.Cars.FirstOrDefault(s => s.Vin == vin);

    if (vehicle == null)
    {
        vehicle = _vehicleContext.Trucks.FirstOrDefault(s => s.Vin == vin);

        if (vehicle != null)
        {
            _vehicleContext.Trucks.Remove((Truck)vehicle);
            _vehicleContext.SaveChanges();
            return;
        }
    }
    else
    {
        _vehicleContext.Cars.Remove((Car)vehicle);
        _vehicleContext.SaveChanges();
        return;
    }

    throw new Exception($"Vehicle does not exist with VIN {vin}");
}
```

The next method is the *GetVehicle()* method. This method will be used to retrieve the *IVehicle* object using the vehicle identification number. The method has one parameter, which is obviously the *VIN* from which the particular object is to be found. First, we are declaring the *IVehicle* variable. The value of this variable is not instantiated, it is just declared, so this variable state is just null for now. Then, we are searching in the database context, in the *Cars* database set, the first-or-default object whose *Vin* property is equal to the **vin** value passed from the parameter. The value returned from this query statement will be stored in the **vehicle** variable. If there is no *Car* object with that particular vin value, the state of the vehicle variable will stay null. If that is the case, we will then search in the *Trucks* database set from the context. The returned value will be stored again in the vehicle variable. If this query also did not return anything but null, the program will throw an exception with the message that there is no vehicle in the database with the provided identification number. However, if there is a vehicle with this particular identification number in the *Cars* or *Trucks* database sets, it will be returned as a result of this method execution.

The next method that is implemented is the *SellVehicle()* method. It also has one parameter, and that parameter is again the vehicle identification number, just like in the previous method. The idea is similar to the previous method; we will search for the vehicle with the provided *vin* inside the database sets, and if any is found, we will remove it from the database set and save the changes. In the beginning, we are declaring the *IVehicle* type variable. Then we search for the vehicle with provided *vin* inside the *Cars* database set. The result is stored in the vehicle variable. If the vehicle is null—no *Car* is found with that identification number, then we will search inside the *Trucks* database set. If the vehicle is found inside the *Trucks* set, we will remove it from the context and execute the *SaveChanges()* over the context. This method assures that the object is deleted from the context. After all these conditions are fulfilled, we will then return the control to the caller of the method.

The other case will be if the vehicle is found inside the *Cars* database set. In this scenario, we are removing the vehicle from the *Cars* context and then performing the *SaveChanges()* method over the context object. If none of the conditions are fulfilled, the program will throw an exception with the message that states that there is no vehicle with the provided identification number. In this scenario, the vehicle is impossible to sell (remove) because the vehicle does not exist at all. Let's take a look at the last method inside the *DealershipService* class:

```csharp
public void AddVehicleToInventory(IVehicle vehicle)
{
    if (vehicle.GetType() == typeof(Car))
    {
        var car = new
Car(vehicle.IsAutomatic,vehicle.Vin,((Car)vehicle).TrunkSpace);

        _vehicleContext.Cars.Add(car);
        _vehicleContext.SaveChanges();
        return;

    }else if (vehicle.GetType() == typeof(Truck))
    {
        var truck = new Truck(vehicle.IsAutomatic, vehicle.Vin,
((Truck)vehicle).BedSpace);
        _vehicleContext.Trucks.Add(truck);
        _vehicleContext.SaveChanges();
        return;
    }

    throw new Exception("Vehicle must be of type Car or Truck");
    }
}
```

The last method implemented is the *AddVehicleToInventory()* method. This method takes one parameter that is an *IVehicle* type object. The first thing that we do here is to check whether the passed vehicle object is of a *Car* class type. If this is correct, the program enters the *if* body block code. Inside this code block, we are instantiating a *Car* class object by providing the *IsAutomatic*, *Vin*, and *TrunkSpace* property values from the passed object. This will invoke the constructor of the *Car* class, and it will create an instance of that object. This object will be stored in the **car** variable. After this, there is an adding of the *car* object to the *Cars* database set inside the database context. This will put a newly created car inside the database set, and then execute the *SaveChanges()* method over the context. The *Cars* set will be increased by one new car. If all of this is done, we return from the function.

The other case is if the vehicle passed object is of the *Truck* class type. In this case, we will instantiate the *Truck* object by providing the *IsAutomatic*, *Vin*, and *BedSpace* property values from the parameter object. This will invoke the *Truck* constructor, and it will return a new object of a *Truck* type to the **truck** variable. After that, the truck is added to the *Trucks* database set inside the context, and the *SaveChanges()* is executed to save the newly added object to the database. After this, we are returning the control to the caller thread. If none of these is executed, the exception is thrown. This exception contains the message that there is no corresponding type for the object parameter passed in—it is neither the *Car* nor *Truck* class type.

This is the whole implementation of the *DealershipService* class, and now we can jump to the other service class implementation:

```
class ManufacturerService:IManufacturerService
{
    public IVehicle BuyVehicle()
    {
        Random randomNumberGenerator = new Random();

        if (randomNumberGenerator.Next(0, 10) % 2 == 0)
        {
            return new Car(true, Guid.NewGuid().ToString(),
randomNumberGenerator.Next(100,499));
        }

        return new Truck(true, Guid.NewGuid().ToString(),
randomNumberGenerator.Next(501,2000));
    }
}
```

The second service class is the *ManufacturerService* class. This class implements the *IManufacturerService* interface, which means that it must have the implementation of the *BuyVehicle()* method. The *BuyVehicle()* method is the method that should return the object of *IVehicle* type to the caller. At the beginning of the method, there is a creation

168

of the object of a *Random* class. In the C#, the *Random* class is the pseudo-random number generator. This means that inside this class, there are methods that produce a sequence of numbers that meet certain criteria. There is a random number generator algorithm implemented here, and it works with providing the statistical requirements for randomness. When buying a vehicle, this method will decide whether that would be a *Car* or a *Truck* vehicle object. The decision will be random.

In the *if* statement, you can see the call for the *Next()* method over the **randomNumberGenerator** object. This object has two parameters provided, the two integer values which represent the minimum and the maximum number to be generated by this method. So, the *Next()* method from *Random* class in C# is generating the random value between provided values. This will generate the number between zero, and then do the modulo operation over it. If the result is an even number, the program will enter the *if* statement body block. So, the even number will result in *Car* object creation, and the odd number will result in *Truck* object creation. The chance for both is about 50-50 percent.

In the scenario where we are creating a *Car* object, we will pass the true value for *IsAutomatic* property, thereby creating a new *GUID* for the vehicle identification number and generating a random value between 100 and 499 for the *TrunkSpace*. If you are not familiar with *GUID* representation, a *GUID* stands for the globally unique identifier, which is also referred to as UUID (universally unique identifier). These numbers are used in the programming world to represent unique numbers because they are almost impossible to repeat while generating. It is a 128-bit reference number. In the case of creating the *Truck* object, we are passing the true value for *IsAutomatic* property, generating a new *GUID* for the vehicle identification number (like in the Car object creation), and passing the value between 501 and 2000 for the *BedSpace* property of a *Truck* class. There is a 50% chance for returning the *Car* object, as well as the *Truck* object as a result of the *BuyVehicle()* method.

Now we can go ahead and see the *Main()* method implementation in the *Program* class, which will put all of this together:

```csharp
static void Main(string[] args)
{
    var options = new DbContextOptionsBuilder<VehicleContext>()
        .UseInMemoryDatabase(databaseName: "VehicleDatabase")
        .Options;

    using (var context = new VehicleContext(options))
    {
        var serviceProvider = new ServiceCollection()
            .AddSingleton<IDealershipService>(s => ActivatorUtilities.CreateInstance<DealershipService>(s, context))
            .AddSingleton<IManufacturerService, ManufacturerService>()
            .BuildServiceProvider();

        string userInput = String.Empty;

        while (userInput != "exit")
        {
            Console.Clear();
            Console.WriteLine("Dealership Manager 2.0");
            Console.WriteLine("Options: \n 1) Buy a vehicle \n 2) Sell a Vehicle \n 3) Show Inventory");
            Console.WriteLine("Choose an option and press enter:");
            userInput = Console.ReadLine();

            if (userInput == "exit")
            {
                break;
            }

            int userInputChoice = Convert.ToInt32(userInput);
            IManufacturerService manufacturerService = serviceProvider.GetService<IManufacturerService>();
            IDealershipService dealershipService = serviceProvider.GetService<IDealershipService>();
```

170

```csharp
if (userInputChoice == 1)
{

    var vehicle = manufacturerService.BuyVehicle();
    dealershipService.AddVehicleToInventory(vehicle);

}else if (userInputChoice == 2)
{
    var vehicle = dealershipService.GetInventory().FirstOrDefault();
    if (vehicle != null)
    {
        dealershipService.SellVehicle(vehicle.Vin);
    }
    else
    {
        Console.WriteLine("You have no vehicles to sell");
    }

}else if (userInputChoice == 3)
{
    var vehicles = dealershipService.GetInventory();
    if (vehicles.Any())
    {
        Console.WriteLine("Here the the VIN numbers for your vehicles");
        vehicles.ForEach(vehicle =>
        {

            Console.WriteLine($"{vehicle.Vin}");

        });
    }
    else
    {
        Console.WriteLine("You do not own any vehicles");
    }


}

Console.WriteLine("Press enter to continue");
userInput = Console.ReadLine();
        }
    }
}
```

The implementation of the *Main()* method is ready to put to life every component in the application now. Let's start. The first thing you notice is the creation of the *DbContextOptionsBuilder* object over which we will use the in-memory database. The Options property of this builder is passed to the options variable because we will need it for the creation of the database context. After this, there is the **using** statement in which we create the context. Next, we will enter the using statement code block, one larger code block where the whole logic will happen. In the beginning, we will initialize the *serviceProvider* variable. We will create a new *ServiceCollection* object and add the required mapping for dependencies. A singleton dependency map is added for both of the service classes. The *DealershipService* mapping is added just with the different overload method *AddSingleton()*, while the singleton service is added with the factory, which is specified as a built-in delegate.

171

After the dependency injection mappings are defined, the *BuildServiceProvider()* method is called over the *ServiceCollection* creation. It prepares everything for the usage of dependency injection. The DI defined mappings will be stored in the *serviceProvider* variable, and we will use that variable to get a particular service when needed. Then we will create one string variable *userInput* and assign an empty string to it. This variable will be responsible for the user interaction with the console application. The *while* loop is executed until the *userInput* variable becomes *"exit"*.

Now, everything is ready for printing the initial state on the console output. We are going to print the options that the user could execute inside the application. First, we are clearing the console, and then we print the console application name in the beginning - "Dealership Manager 2.0." The options for the user will be: 1) Buy a vehicle 2) Sell a vehicle 3) Show inventory. The user is able to communicate with the application by pressing the one, two, or three value in the console. When the user presses any of these numbers on the keyboard, the value will be stored inside the *userInput* variable *(userInput = Console.ReadLine())*. If the user types *"exit"* to the console line, the program will break, and the execution will finish. If the user types the number *1* and presses enter, the program will execute the first *if* statement code block. If the user presses the number *1* and enter, it means that they want to perform the action of buying a car. So, we are calling the *serviceProvider* to get the *IManufacturerService* type service and to execute the *BuyVehicle()* method over that service object. This method execution will create one random instance of the *Car* or the *Truck* class objects and return that value. It will be stored in the vehicle variable.

Now, when a vehicle is bought, we must store it inside the inventory. So, we call the *serviceProvider* to resolve the *IDealershipService* type and to get the *DealershipService* object over which we will execute the *AddVehicleToInventory()* method, passing the previously bought vehicle. This will determine whether the passed parameter vehicle is of the *Car* or *Truck* class type. After that, it will put it inside one of the database sets and save the new *Car* instance to the database.

The second user choice could be to sell a vehicle. This will happen if the user types the number *2* and presses enter. This will lead the program into the second *if* statement in which the program needs to perform the selling of a vehicle. The first thing that must be done here is the retrieval of all the vehicles. This is done by calling the *serviceProvider* to resolve the *IDealershipService* type to get the service over which it will execute the *GetInventory()* method. This will return all the vehicles inside the inventory, and then the *FirstOrDefault()* Entity Framework Core extension method could be executed. This will take the first element inside the inventory if the inventory is not empty and store it inside the vehicle variable. If the vehicle is not null, and the inventory was not empty, that means that we can perform the selling of the car. We will do that by calling the *serviceProvider* to resolve a service object and then call the *SellVehicle()* method over it.

In this call, we will pass the *Vin* property value of the vehicle variable so the program can know the vehicle to remove from the database set. This will search for the vehicle in the *Cars* database set first; if found, it will remove it from the set; if not, the program will perform the search over the *Trucks* database set. Furthermore, if the vehicle is found there, the removal will be executed over the Trucks set. If there were no vehicles in the inventory, the program would print the message, *"You have no vehicles to sell"* onto the console output.

The last case left is the number *3* input. If the user types the number *3* and presses enter, it means that he wants to see his inventory listed in the program. All the cars he bought should appear there in the list. The first thing we should do is to get all the vehicles from the inventory if there are any and store them inside a variable. In order to do this, we will need to call the *serviceProvider* to resolve the *IDealershipService* once again and to get the service object. When this is done, we will then execute the *GetInventory()* method over that service object. This will return the list of vehicles in the inventory and store them into the vehicle's variable. Then we have a check if there are any elements in the vehicles variable list.

If the condition is true, we must print the vehicles to the user, and the user is then informed that the list will contain the vehicle identification numbers. Then we will iterate through each vehicle in the vehicles list and print the *Vin* property value of the vehicle to the console output. If there were no vehicles in the inventory, the user would get the message *"You do not own any vehicles"* on the standard output. To confirm any of the actions, the user must press enter in the end, and then, the loop will start again. With this solution, we have managed to make an interactive application that communicates with the user via the console input.

Now let's test this application. We will start it and act as a user. The console will look like this in the beginning:

```
C:\Users\LENOVO\Desktop\EBOOK C#\EBOOK C#\Outline Problem Examples\CarDealershipManager\bin\Debug\netcoreapp3.1\CarDealershipManage...    —    □    ×
Dealership Manager 2.0
Options:
 1) Buy a vehicle
 2) Sell a Vehicle
 3) Show Inventory
Choose an option and press enter:
```

We will first test the edge case. We will then choose the *"Sell a vehicle"* option—
Number *2*. It should print the message that we do not own any vehicles. Let's try it and
see what happens:

```
C:\Users\LENOVO\Desktop\EBOOK C#\EBOOK C#\Outline Problem Examples\CarDealershipManager\bin\Debug\netcoreapp3.1\CarDealershipManage...    —    □    ×
Dealership Manager 2.0
Options:
 1) Buy a vehicle
 2) Sell a Vehicle
 3) Show Inventory
Choose an option and press enter:
2
You have no vehicles to sell
Press enter to continue
```

Good! Now, let's try to buy three vehicles. We will execute the option one three times:

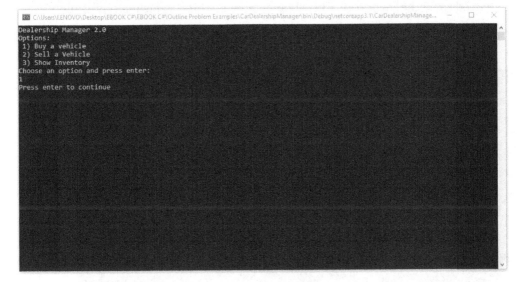

Now, let's try to display the inventory. This should show us three vehicle identification numbers because we have purchased three vehicles:

Great, there are three vehicles in our possession. Now let's sell one vehicle and show the inventory again. It should display two vehicle identification numbers.

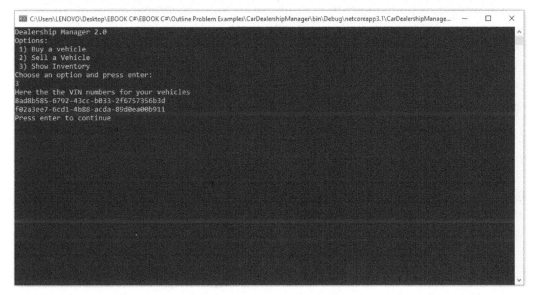

Great! Everything is working correctly!

Chapter 10: Conclusion

Congratulations! You have read the whole book and made your first step towards mastering the C# programming language. This book described the basic knowledge you should have in order to start evolving with C# and the .NET runtime. It is important that you have understood all of the examples presented in this book. This would mean that you obtained high-quality knowledge for a beginner. If you did not understand all of the examples, we would suggest that you go back and read the section again, attempt to search the internet for the answer, or even ask someone who has some programming experience. After that, you are ready to start improving your algorithmic thinking, as well as advance your C# programming skills. After you advance passed the skills presented in this book, remember to continue to read more advanced books about C#, search the internet for answers, and ask other programmers because the C# ecosystem changes at a rapid pace and you will gain more advanced skill sets that are desirable to employers.

If you want to practice programming in C# beyond the examples provided in this book, you could look up one of the many open source C# projects on the internet and attempt to volunteer on the project, or create your own project and possibly submit it on one of the many public source repositories as an open source project. If you do, attempt to find an issue, request, or problem just around the edge of your ability and attempt to master it.

This programming language is one of the most popular and modern programming languages in the world. It's not hard to learn if you're going step by step and trying to understand everything with high concentration and hard work. There are several support options for C# to make everything more comfortable, as you can find many solutions for different problems across the internet. This will help you develop your skills at a faster rate. C# can be used in almost any kind of software development such as Console Applications, Mobile Applications, Web Services, Windows Applications, Blockchain Development, Cloud Applications, Artificial Intelligence, Machine Learning, etc. It is on you to choose your passion and start improving in a particular field. We hope you enjoyed this book, don't stop, and keep up the good work!